Guéridon and Lamp Cookery

By the same author

The Chef's Manual of Kitchen Management
The Caterer's Potato Manual
Catering Management in the Technological Age
Modern Restaurant Service

With E. Renold
The Chef's Compendium of Professional Recipes

With A. J. Currie
The Waiter

With D. A. C. Gee
Hotel and Institutional Housekeeping
A Career in Hotels and Catering

Three important items of equipment for cooking
and service from the guéridon. *Left*, the traditional chafing dish with ebony handle and complete with stand and lamp (its twin-handled spare
dish is in the foreground). *Centre*, the *presse* for
canard à la presse, and *Right*, the "lamp" of the
kind now commonly used, topped by a lipped
blazer or Suzette pan. This model is spirit operated, but butane gas models of similar appearance
are now gaining in popularity.

Guéridon and Lamp Cookery

John Fuller

Hutchinson
London Melbourne Sydney Auckland Johannesburg

Hutchinson & Co. (Publishers) Ltd

An imprint of the Hutchinson Publishing Group

17-21 Conway Street, London W1P 6JD

Hutchinson Group (Australia) Pty Ltd
30-32 Cremorne Street, Richmond South, Victoria 3121
PO Box 151, Broadway, New South Wales 2007

Hutchinson Group (NZ) Ltd
32-34 View Road, PO Box 40-086, Glenfield, Auckland 10

Hutchinson Group (SA) (Pty) Ltd
PO Box 337, Bergvlei 2012, South Africa

First published by Barrie & Jenkins 1964
Reprinted 1965 and 1972
Second edition 1975
Reprinted 1978
First published by Hutchinson 1980
Reprinted 1982 and 1984

Printed and bound in Great Britain by
Anchor Brendon Ltd, Tiptree, Essex

ISBN 0 09 141390 7

CONTENTS

ILLUSTRATIONS

FOREWORD

This guide has been prepared to assist professional restaurateurs and waiting staff but in the belief that considerations of guéridon and flambé services are by no means confined solely to the largest and most luxurious establishments.

Recipes and procedures which are a preliminary part of dishes and of service but which are normally carried out by the chef in the kitchen have, in general, either been abbreviated or omitted (except for a brief reference). In one or two cases, however, fuller detailing of kitchen preparation has been provided, chiefly for the two following reasons. First, to aid the smaller restaurant proprietor who may wish to introduce a dish not previously served such as *suprême de volaille sous cloche*, but secondly to give the guéridon operative background explanation which gives better understanding of his own part and enables him (if called upon) to pass this on to the guest. It has, however, been assumed that those who aspire to undertake guéridon and flambé work already have some knowledge of waiting and some acquaintanceship with the basics of cookery.

Though designed for professionals practising restaurant service, the guide has been compiled with thought also to the needs of those still undertaking training; particularly waiting apprentices in hotels and restaurants and also students in hotel schools and the catering departments of technical colleges. The needs have been borne in mind of those preparing for the Final Examination in Waiting of the Hotel and Catering Institute, for the National Diploma in Hotel and Catering Subjects and for the Membership examination of the Hotel and Catering Institute.

Acknowledgements

I wish to acknowledge the help given in preparing parts of this manual by lecturing staff of the Scottish Hotel School including

Mr A. J. Currie, maître d'hôtel lecturer and Mr Charles Jarvie, sous chef lecturer, who both read and checked one or two chapters during its preparation. I am especially grateful to Mr Joseph Houston, lecturer in restaurant service, for similar reading and checking and also for his assistance in helping to prepare procedures for illustrations.

I also thank Mr H. R. Freeman for contributing two recipes and Mr George Mulvey for specialities which he has devised and featured in the Boulevard Hotel, Glasgow.

I also acknowledge with gratitude the generosity of Messrs Gilbey Ltd. for providing the pictures which illustrate this manual and also for supplying brandy and other liquors used in making the dishes portrayed.

I am also indebted to British Silverware Ltd for permission to quote from their instructions in the use of their gas operated table lamp and to reproduce line diagrams of the Savoy lamp.

In expressing thanks to those who so kindly assisted me when this book was in preparation, I would stress that responsibility for its contents and for any errors or omissions are mine alone.

Glasgow, 1964.   JOHN FULLER

CHAPTER I

AIMS AND CONSIDERATIONS AFFECTING GUÉRIDON AND LAMP COOKERY

Since the Edwardian period flambé dishes have played an increasingly important role in restaurants catering for prosperous sections of society. Whether or not one queries the anecdote of the young commis waiter setting on fire by accident the prototype of a long sequence of crêpes Suzette when busying himself to please the Prince of Wales, who later became Edward VII, there is no doubt that the little fires of those days have been spreading like a forest blaze through restaurants of the western world ever since.

Demand for "Seen Service"

Flambé work is an extension and elaboration of guéridon and side-table service and this kind of attention is so long established that its origins are less easy to pinpoint than the beginnings of guéridon work. Carving, salad preparation and the finishing of fruit and desserts are amongst those aspects of side-table service that give opportunity for flair and display by the maître d'hôtel and waiter. Guéridon service including flambé work, whatever their domestic or hotel origins, today meet clear and basic requirements from the points of view both of the guest and restaurateur.

Indeed, from the guest's standpoint, it is a particular manifestation in catering today at whatever level that there is a strong sympathy with "seen service". The modest griddling of hamburgers or pizzas in a coffee bar or snack service has at its own level the same kind of visual appeal that more elaborate forms of lamp cookery have in luxury establishments. As more and more people eat out there is an increased demand for "something different" from the catering they receive at home (or in the factory or at school). This is further linked with that substantial element amongst the restaurateurs' patrons at all levels who dine out to "escape" and who seek not merely release from domestic chores but a positive element of entertainment. Chinese style ovens in Trader Vic's are claimed to be ideal for cooking but additionally they have this strong element of visual interest.

This trend to move cookery into the dining area or at least where the cooking processes may be seen by the guests though it is revealed at quite modest levels in rôtisseries, barbecue and griddle services, and where part of the appeal may depend upon gadgets and white-garbed chefs, nevertheless strongly suggests that customers in higher class restaurants will continue to appreciate and demand similar visual services; in particular, individual seen-service at the guéridon and on the lamp. Moreover, there is particular fascination for many in "guest participation" services of which fondue and self-prepared dressings are indicative of general trends.

Selling

The inclusion, here and there, amongst recipes and amongst suggestions for guéridon and lamp work of anecdotes and even historical information is not thought to be inappropriate. Excessive chattiness from a maître d'hôtel or waiter is to be deplored but there may be occasions when a little background comment about the dish being prepared, about its origins, points about the commodities used and even the dish's history or historical associations may be of interest. Indeed, intelligent comment about a dish listed on the menu or featured as a house speciality can be regarded as a point in its promotion.

"Selling" a dish can hardly be achieved by blatant or vulgar means but a display of interest by a proprietor and his staff in their craft and its background generally, or a specific dish in particular, is likely to be communicated to a guest. To evoke from a guest an interested response should not be without benefit in promoting a restaurant's business. Solid sales will, however, only continuously result from good, tasty dishes deftly and pleasantly served.

Restaurateurs who may wonder from time to time as to the solidity, as it were, of operations that exploit guéridon and flambé work will have regard to the clearly evidenced desires of their guests for such forms of service. They will moreover seldom be slow to see that visual and dramatic presentations are powerful aids in promoting business. Guests are impressed by the skills shown in guéridon performances. Flambé-ing, in particular, is a reliable means of attracting the attention of other tables in a restaurant, and has the effect of provoking repeat orders. Above all, the flickering lamp, the gleaming silver, the mise en place on the side table add substantially to restaurant atmosphere and help create an ambience both different from home and expected when eating out.

Such considerations are not by any means dependent merely on the present affluence of society nor the free spending at expense account meals, but are amongst the fundamental reasons for eating out.

Individualism and Change

The chapters which follow, therefore, seek to treat of the basic sections of guéridon and flambé work as substantial and enduring parts of professional catering at top level. Top level does not necessarily mean inevitably the most expensive or the most fabulously decorated eating places; for many of the aspects of table cooking and forms of service may be, and probably will continue to be, increasingly developed in restaurants where a proprietor or manager seeks to give an individual touch to the food and service he offers his guest. That there is an element of gimmick and of transient fashion in so far as the odd dish may be concerned there can be little doubt. But so far as restaurant operation in general is concerned, the fundamentals of side-table cookery and service have already persisted for at least half a century and are likely to persist for at least as long again.

The maître d'hôtel in a large, smart restaurant and the restaurateur or chef proprietor in a smaller city or country establishment must, therefore, continue to find a modern relevance in much of the guéridon tradition. Happily, this tradition is one which calls, and calls vigorously, for individualism, for change and for progress.

Controversy surrounding Flaming

Straightforward guéridon service such as carving, salad making and dessert composing is universally praised not only for promotional appeal on business grounds but by guests, gourmets and professional restaurateurs alike as fulfilling the best conditions of gastronomy. Side-table cookery particularly flambé work is, on the other hand, much more controversial from an epicurean point of view even though its merchandising value is generally acknowledged. Many gastronomes consider that cooking should be left to the chef in the kitchen and that an amalgam of culinary smells (not excluding meths. from the lamp) are not desirable in the restaurant.

This manual does not seek to arbitrate between those who adore and those who abhor flambé cookery, but accepts that it is bound to remain and that the professional in the hotel and restaurant business must bring maximum skills and maximum enthusiasm and interest to bear on it. Perhaps some restaurateurs, especially in the New World, have brought excessive enthusiasm and zeal to flambé work and there is undoubtedly danger in seeking to expand unduly the repertoire of flared dishes. Some foods and some processes are clearly unsuitable for side-table cookery and extravagances should not be dragged in merely to achieve something different.

The specific sections of the book which deal with flambé savoury dishes and flambé sweet dishes themselves give guidance in table cookery and flaming principles, but it may be as well to note here and at the outset some of the basic considerations for flaming.

Points to observe in Flaming

Chapter 3 on *Liquors and Commodities* makes it apparent that most liquids having noticeable alcoholic content are capable of being flamed once the alcohol is vaporising. Obviously, however, those with higher alcohol content will do so more easily.

To be able to flame a fortified wine such as sherry means keeping it undiluted and having it vesselled for flaming (in dish, spoon or ladle) in a warm (often, indeed, in a heated) condition.

Even in the case of the stronger spirits and liqueurs it is important not to allow the flambé-ing liquid to become diluted with sauce, syrup or *jus* until it is well alight.

It is, further, vital to ignite quickly on the liquor's addition.

Flame by touching the liquor's vapour to the lamp flame and never with a match.

Once flambé-ing is in process stirring promotes the blaze and basting is, therefore, more effective and spectacular if done when the pan is afire.

Sugar sprinkled into the blaze in sweet dishes varies the flame colour.

Extinguish the flames by smothering with the lid or blanketing with cream or sauce.

Remember that flaming has little or no effect on the heat of food dressed in the flambé sauce or liquor; thus the food must first be adequately cooked and be piping hot.

Appearance and Hygiene

Because this book deals with particular and specialised facets of restaurant service many of the general factors of service have naturally been excluded. One important aspect must, however, be stressed right at the beginning. This aspect is of hygiene and of personal appeal. More than anything else individual service and cooking at the guéridon hinges upon the personality and appearance of the maître d'hôtel or waiter who performs the service. Good manners, pleasant speech, smart appearance, scrupulous grooming and cleanliness are basic needs and should be given emphasis before all the technical skills which follow.

An underlying factor which gives appeal to guéridon work is that it can be such a strong confidence builder. Everything going into the dish or everything that is to be served can be clearly seen and can be freshly prepared. Yet all this confidence can be destroyed if the person giving the service has untrimmed and dirty finger nails, nicotine staining on the fingers, soiled shirt cuffs, spotted jacket and so on. But questions of hygiene do not end there; and mouth and body hygiene when the service is given so near to the guest also assumes dominant importance.

So often one notes that an otherwise well-groomed waiter will have a loose lock of hair falling as he bends and busies himself at service. Unthinkingly brushing back hair with the hands and then returning to serve sets up intense reaction from the guest even though hair and hands may appear to be clean. Because of the limitations of this manual's main subject it is not appropriate to detail every point in personal hygiene, but suffice it to say that those who are to perform at the lamp must give scrupulous attention to hygiene.

Even the ordinary waiter or waitress because they are in uniform and are moving about in a public place attract far more attention to themselves than workers in most other fields of activity. When their duties involve them in more dramatised presentations, such as in flambé work, then the attention they attract obviously tends to be even greater. All the extra promotional appeal of guéridon and flambé work does not mask or cover personal or operational deficiencies elsewhere in the restaurant. Indeed, the contribution guéridon and flambé work demands, calls for even greater emphasis on the fundamental qualities of good waiters and good waiting.

CHAPTER 2

EQUIPMENT AND STAFF

The large and leading hotels of the world have long offered permutations on the two basic forms of menu, *à la carte* and *table d'hôte* and have varied their forms of service to support them. The old Silver Grill and the present-day grill rooms which often develop into a form indistinguishable from an à la carte restaurant certainly have been elaborated in recent years. Alternatively, they have been supported by additional speciality restaurants in which exotic dishes and exotic décor have underlined the fact that for many guests dining out is a quest for entertainment just as much as a need to satisfy appetite.

Guéridon Service and Staff
Service from the guéridon has tended to be associated increasingly with à la carte service or with elaboration of à la carte service as found in speciality restaurants; but guéridon work is by no means out of place in the normal table d'hôte service of a large hotel or a top class restaurant conducted in the classic tradition.

Moreover, even in "popular" catering operations an element of guéridon service has been a noticeable feature in recent years. Restaurants appealing at medium price range have, by confining choice to a few "highlighted" dishes, found it possible to train waiting staff to higher levels, albeit in a much narrower field of work.

It is, for example, commonplace to see side-table treatment of salads and *pommes au four* (baked jacket potatoes) by a waitress but her skill would certainly not be expected to extend further to, for example, guéridon filleting of sole or the carving of a chicken. It

7

will be apparent, therefore, that the application of side-table service can and does vary considerably according to the scope and intention of the operation.

In the classic French restaurant whether operating table d'hôte or à la carte services a sign of quality has, however, been the extent to which individual finishing at the moment of service is given. Thus high class service has long been associated with maximum exploitation of guéridon techniques.

The traditional restaurant brigade was (and where it remains in existence, still is) well adapted for this form of service. The restaurant heirarchy from the maître d'hôtel down through reception head waiter, station head waiters, chef de rang, commis de rang, commis de suite, commis débarrasseur, afford the facilities for a high degree of individual waiter attention at table. The essence of effective side-table work is, indeed, the support of the station head waiter or of the chef de rang by assistants. The action of the commis waiters in bringing dishes from the servery and in clearing away unwanted items permits the chef de rang waiter to concentrate his attention on the mise en place both on his sideboard and on the guéridon prepared for the service of dishes. Without assistant waiters it is virtually impossible to give full guéridon service and even partial guéridon service would be a slow and tedious affair without those to fetch and carry for the main operator. In large restaurants, therefore, the size of the brigade, the amount of equipment and the increased time, involve higher operational costs which must inevitably be reflected in prices charged to the guest.

Choice of Equipment

For most restaurants initiating a new operation there will be a choice as to the range and extent of side-table work and whether this is to be concentrated on the main parts of the menu or is to run right through it. A restaurateur's decisions and policy will naturally have regard to prices to be charged, clientele to be attracted, availability of staff and other factors. His final choice will not affect all items equally for the basic components of silver service such as oval and round silver flats, entrée and vegetable dishes, timbales and so on for sweets will be required whether dishes are presented to guests in French or English service or used from the side table. For flambé work and special services there must, however, be some widening of the general range of items required in the restaurant.

The Guéridon or Side Table

Originally meaning in France a small table with a single central pedestal (see also the glossary), the word guéridon has now acquired special significance in the restaurant world. One American training manual (*The Essentials of Good Table Service*, Cornell University) refers to a "guéridon (cart)" but mobility through wheels though often a desirable convenience is adding a new and not necessarily a more helpful or accurate significance to the term guéridon. Others have suggested that a guéridon must be equipped with a lamp, réchaud or hotplate to distinguish it from a side table. In fact, however, to most restaurateurs the words guéridon and side table have precisely the same meaning.

As the guéridon or side table should be movable the simple, small table which was lifted bodily to adjoin the guests' table when service was required has undergone development so that nowadays table-height trolleys are also designated guéridons. They are, indeed, often sufficiently elaborate to have "built in" lamps, an underleaf shelf or second level and other features. Such elaborations of the guéridon seem, perhaps, inappropriately translated by the English term "side table" but they remain, of course, work points for "side table" service, carving and cooking.

Simple side tables without wheels must remain quite small to be easily movable though they are seldom less than $1\frac{1}{2}$ ft. by 2 ft. surface size. Any side table or voiture used for guéridon service should be the same height as the restaurant table but surface area tends to vary according to the needs of the service and the opinion of the restaurateur.

Some waiters favour side tables that are partially wheeled with large casters or small wheels on two legs of the four. Carts or voitures used as guéridons, with all four legs wheeled have the advantage of being easily mobile even when they have larger work surfaces and consequently their usage is increasing.

In one middle eastern country at a time when there were some import difficulties, a restaurant had "mocked up" an improvised voiture from wrought iron into which was fixed clips to hold a "picnic" type butane gas flare lamp from which effective flambé work and guéridon cookery could be achieved.

Trolleys

In considering staff and equipment required for this type of work it can, of course, be noted that devices such as the trolley may provide for guéridon service. They can also do so on a multiple scale. The hors d'œuvres trolley, the heated trolley for the carving and serving of large joints, the dessert and salad trolleys and even the liqueur trolley are simply extensions of the guéridon principle of bringing food for service to the side of the guest's table. They have additionally a sales promotional value in visually encouraging the guest to choose features of the day. They aid impulse buying.

As was noted above, trolleys specifically devised and manufactured for flambé work are also being increasingly used in many countries.

Table Cooking Lamps

First and foremost to be considered amongst guéridon items is the "lamp" itself. It must be stressed that the lamp should correctly be regarded as an appliance primarily designed for cooking or certainly for positive reheating as distinct from simply keeping foods warm. The true restaurateur deplores the abuse of the lamp merely as a means of ensuring that items from the kitchen which should have been hot in the first instance are made so. For example, vegetables which should be prepared and cooked by the chef in the kitchen to a precise degree of excellence are readily spoiled by further, incorrect and unnecessary cooking on the réchaud. The lamp is not, therefore, a substitute for a sideboard hotplate either electrically heated or spirit lamp heated nor is it a device to mask deficiencies in the service of hot items.

Lamps are relatively costly items but it is, nevertheless, essential that the restaurant is adequately furnished with them if flambé work is to become anything of a feature. It is important that each station head waiter or each chef de rang responsible for lamp work is assigned, if possible, at least one lamp for his own exclusive use. Not only does this obviate delay and possible dispute between stations but also has clear advantages in the interest and care taken by the waiter concerned in the maintenance and cleanliness of this piece of apparatus.

A silver plated or hotel plated traditional style lamp today is likely to cost between upwards of £35 for a spirit lamp and up-

wards of £45 for a butane gas model. They are made in more than
one size but are usually about 8 in. to 10 in. in height and with a
grid diameter of 6 in. to 8 in. It is sometimes possible to find one
or two secondhand and reconditioned models in, for example,
silversmiths and suppliers in Soho who specialise in caterers' requirements. Drakes Silversmiths, Ltd., 49 Brewer Street, London,
W.1, a family firm who specialise in restaurant equipment and
plating, often recondition catering and table requipment of all
kinds. Additionally, British Silverware Ltd. (which comprises
Mappin, Elkington and Walker and Hall) with head office at
21 Terminal House, Grosvenor Gardens, London, S.W.1, have a
wide range of new items.

In America and other parts of the world réchaud lamps have
been manufactured and are widely used in newer outward forms.
There are many lower priced and simpler models including a particularly useful variety provided with a handle attached to the base
for easy handling. Copper and other metals are also being used in
place of the hotel plated finish.

Smaller Spirit Stoves and Fondue Stands

As distinct from true restaurant "lamps" quite simple spirit stoves
in brass and black metal, for example, are now obtainable at
£5–£7 but such types are perhaps less well suited for the
rigours of use by waiters unless reserved for fondue service.

For fondue service there have been simple adaptations of stoves
and lamps consisting of little more than a tripod into which a night
light type flame of candle may be fitted. This has enabled kitchen
prepared fondue to be served in batches of individual servings for
much larger parties.

Some types of fondue apparatus, though of attractive appearance, are too fragile for catering use, and restaurateurs who are
tempted by domestic strength equipment may regret it when they
see the results of staff handling.

Chafing Dish

The true chafing dish is relatively seldom seen in modern restaurant operations. The original type of chafing dish differed from
the lamp and crêpe pan. The chafing dish or pan is deeper, provided with a lid and is, of course, made precisely to fit its own
individual heating unit. In fact, the chafing dish was originally

designed for dishes requiring forms of cooking additional to quick
sauté-ing and flambé-ing and few restaurants either today or in
the past have been prepared to devote the time to a full range of
chafing dish work. The complete appliance has been rather regarded as a domestic cooking apparatus. Chafing dishes may, of
course, be used for fondues though here again the specially devised
fondue units now available are tending to usurp even this role.

The original and true form of the chafing dish apparatus incorporating the lamp itself consists of three principal parts:

    1. The frame or stand in which the lamp is mounted and in
or on which the pan or blazer can be placed.
    2. The lamp.
    3. The cooking dishes, pans or blazers in which food may
be heated or cooked.

This latter item does, of course, have variants; for older and some
current models have a bain-marie type pan, i.e. deeper hot water
pan with side handles on to which the blazer may be fitted when
slow cooking is required. Understandably, this has little restaurant
application.

Additionally, there may be provided a round, plated dish sometimes known in the past as the cutlet dish.

The deeper pan, blazer or chafing dish proper usually has a
handle (frequently of ebony) or twin side handles of metal and is
completed by a centre handled lid.

Shallow type pans (of the type nowadays called Suzette pans)
have long been provided for sauté-ing or omelette making.

Complete chafing dish outfits for domestic use have often in
past years been sold complete with special tools, particularly
spoons for stirring and mixing, both wooden and silver plated,
and long handled fork. Some sets even included skimmers and egg
poachers with a special plated flagon for methylated spirits, elegant
enough in style to be kept in the dining room for topping up purposes.

Indeed, chafing dish cookery became highly fashionable at the
end of the nineteenth century, continuing into the Edwardian
period, and the use of the apparatus in private houses may have
been associated (in the United States of America, for example)
with the difficulties of finding and keeping properly trained
domestic staff.

Culinary writer Frank Schloesser whose book *The Chafing Dish* was published in 1904 when the vogue for this sort of cookery in private houses was at its height, whimsically averred that he was wedded to "Chafinda", his chafing dish. More interestingly, he unearthed a reference to the use of a réchaud in de la Varenne's *Le Cuisinier français*, published in 1652. The recipe for which it was used was *Champignons à l'Olivier* and in an English translation, *The French Cook*, published in London in the following year, the reader was similarly advised about the use of a chafing dish for "mushrooms after the Oliver".

Fuel for the Lamp

As recently as the early 1930's many chefs of the old school were so used to solid top ranges that they regarded it as difficult if not impossible to get good results with ranges and cooking equipment using electricity or gas. Nowadays, such an attitude seems incomprehensible and chefs demand the latest type of gas and electric appliances. This may be a pointer to the possible developments in lamps should this type of restaurant service continue to be demanded.

Many maîtres d'hôtel were strongly in favour of lamps using methylated spirits and became thoroughly accustomed to controlling the flame and the heat by adjusting the wick. But apart from this traditional method of heating there are now types of lamp which whilst of conventional external appearance are equipped with compressed gas of butane type. Once the operator is accustomed to "gas lamps" their use offers a well controlled and clean flame well suited to cooking in the room. The gas flame is readily adjusted by movement of the tap in a way similar to that in which the wick screw is turned.

When chafing dish cookery was fashionable during the early years of the century electric models were made, but for speedier types of dishes requiring frequent changes and control of heat electricity has not seemed so appropriate for commercial restaurant use.

Some gourmets deplore the use of lamps for cooking in the room not only because of culinary smells intruding on neighbouring diners at inappropriate stages of their meals but also because of the possible penetration of the odour of methylated spirit. Thus, when spirit lamps are used scrupulous cleanliness and constant wick control is of extreme importance.

Steak Diane Sets and Chafing Dish Variants

Apart from lamps and pans of conventional style and chafing dishes of traditional pattern there are now available (particularly in U.S.A.) lamp sets or chafing dish sets with, for example, rectangular pans or dishes. Such variants may be named Steak Diane sets or some similar term.

Care of Spirit Lamps

During the early part of the day before service starts, and when the restaurant staff should be attending to their menage and mise en place, the lamps must be thoroughly checked to ensure:

1. Cleanliness.
2. That they are charged with methylated spirits (or that replacement gas cylinders are available as appropriate).
3. That the wick is adequate for the forthcoming service period.

For an average lamp of traditional pattern the consumption of methylated spirits, assuming the lamp is kept alight and is used normally over the service period, can be expected to be about one ½ pint per hour, i.e. 1½ pints per 3 hours' service period use. It is apparent that an adequate stock of spirit must be kept and that a reserve be available even during service time.

The following rules should be observed.

1. See that the wicks of the lamp are regularly and properly trimmed.
2. See that the wick is long enough to reach the bottom of the spirit well to make effective contact with, soak up and transmit the spirit. An inadequate wick burning dry may, apart from unpleasant smouldering, burn down and ignite fumes in the spirit well with possibly unpleasant and even explosive results. Sometimes a tight wick may cause initial difficulty in lighting. Prodding through the wick wad with a thin skewer or similar sharp pointed implement is often effective when lighting is difficult.
3. Check that the lamp's spirit container is replenished at the beginning of each service during the menage or mise en place period.

4. In use, control the flame to ensure that it heats the bottom of the blazer or pan and does not flame up by the sides.

Care of the Gas Table Lamp

In using gas operated table cooking lamps, the Savoy model, manufactured by Elkington & Co., Ltd, may be regarded as a typical type. The makers of the Savoy in providing directions for its use stress the following:

1. When fitting a gas container, close the regulating valve. On the Savoy this is effected by turning valve control knob (1) to the right.

2. Screw the gas container (2) firmly into the thread at the base of the valve, ensuring that the sealing washer (3) is in position.

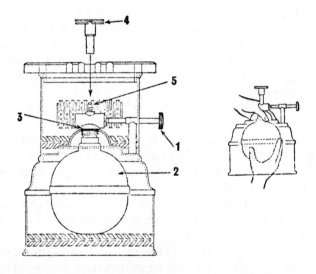

3. Keep the lamp upright whilst tightening. This upright position is essential to prevent the escape of liquid gas. The lamp must always be used in the upright position.

4. Do not attach or detach a gas container near a naked light or flame.

5. When the gas container has been firmly connected to the regulating valve by turning the control knob to the left apply a match to the burner (4).

6. In the event of the jet becoming choked, unscrew the burner from the valve body and remove the jet (5), with the small spanner supplied with each lamp. Blow through the jet at both directions and hold up to the light to make sure that the orifice is clear.

In no circumstances should a pricker be used to clear the jet as this may affect the efficiency of the burner. (A spare jet and a spanner are enclosed with each lamp.)

7. Gas containers should be stored in a cool place when not in use.

8. When cleaning the lamp do not immerse the regulating valve or burner in water.

Hotplates or chauffe-plats

Formerly, chauffe-plats were invariably spirit heated with a portable lamp but nowadays hotplate heating-stands are often electrically heated. Not only are they available in patterns which simulate the traditional spirit heated ones but also come in more modern designs. Electric hotplates are normally positioned permanently on the sideboard.

Hotplate-type heating-stands in which the plate is heated by methylated spirit lamp or similar heating-stands of the same traditional style or of more modern appearance fitted for electricity are made in varying sizes from about 11 × 7 ins. to as large as 26 × 9 ins., this latter size requiring two lamps if traditionally heated.

For guéridon use there are, however, hotplates consisting of heat retaining panels. A number of these may be stacked in a small batterie at a convenient service point inside or outside "the room" and brought either to the side table or to the sideboard for use by the waiter as required. The heating and storage unit accommodates from two to ten plates and fast-heating, infra-red elements ensure a swift and reliable flow of the stands as required. This type of apparatus is tending to replace the small individual units equipped with small night light type candles whose flames heated a small metal sheet on a glass, plastic or other type of container. It is, however, on hotplates as distinct from lamps that reliance should be placed for keeping food warm.

Crêpe Suzette Pan

Plated, shallow fry-pans, blazers or crêpe Suzette pans differ from those traditionally provided in chafing dish sets though in fact at the present time these pans of crêpe Suzette pan type tend to be used by restaurateurs for far more work than flambé-d pancakes. They resemble frying pans in shape and size normally ranging in diameter from 9 ins. to 12 ins. They are obtainable with or without lip, the lip usually being sited on the left hand side when provided. The pans are either wholly plated with silver or hotel plate or, as is much to be preferred, are copper on the outside with the silver or hotel plating confined to the interior surface. Copper, an efficient conductor of heat, enables good spread of heat throughout the pan relatively quickly and effectively. This helps to eliminate the high spot of heat in the centre of the pan which is a common factor in causing burning and irregular cooking. It is as well to have more than one size of pan per station and where pan work is to be a pronounced feature of the operation then more than one should be assigned to each waiter or to each lamp to ensure that there is proper time and opportunity for cleaning.

Similarly, in addition to the round blazer or crêpe Suzette pans there are oval types and as noted above rectangular styles for steak Diane sets.

Tools at the Guéridon

One of the principles of cooking and carving "in the room" is that use should be made only of restaurant cutlery and that cookery implements as such should be avoided. For carving, for example, table knives are normally used for smaller items (prudent waiters naturally retain a well cared for, specially sharpened knife for this purpose) and carvers for larger items. It is, of course, true that chef trancheurs who come into the restaurant to carve at the buffet or meat wagon traditionally may use their own tools, but otherwise standard "restaurant gear" is used by waiters for normal guéridon work.

Shaslik Swords

Flaming sword service has been a feature of American restaurants for many years but until recently so little had these devices been used in Britain that one culinary journal in 1961 reported that the

American owned Carlton Towers Hotel was the only place in Britain then serving flamed meat in this style. This provoked correspondence which revealed that, as in America, swords as skewers were in use in Europe. In Germany, for example, such forms of service had been initiated in 1953 (at the Restaurant Atelier in Cologne). The plain stiletto type swords with crossed handles in the illustrations sent by the German correspondent differed, however, from models often used in America. These have hilts protected by a hollowed guard and also incorporate a second bowl near the hilt end which can contain flambé-ing material or capture juices. Sliding, retaining bolts are also incorporated in many shaslik swords. Purporting to reflect middle eastern or east European traditions, flaming sword service is, in fact, rather a restaurant exploitation of the western world. They may be obtained ready manufactured in the U.S.A. (from Legion Utensils Company Incorporated, 2107 40th Avenue, Long Island City, 1, New York, which specialises in flambé and guéridon equipment), but are still not readily found in Britain. Hotel silversmiths and suppliers can, however, make them to specification.

There are new signs, however, that sword service is on the increase in this country. It is, for example, a main feature of *L'Epée d'Or* (The Golden Sword), the speciality restaurant adjoining the Cumberland Hotel at Marble Arch. The swords there are made by the famous firm of Wilkinson and are mounted into a large circular grill of stainless steel specially made by Benhams for display work in this operation. The venture is a notable experiment in London in merchandising food.

Other Speciality Equipment

Further notes concerning equipment will be found in the section dealing with special services concerned. Shaslik swords, kebab skewers and similar items are further considered, for example, in Chapter 8. Carving tools, salad equipment and seafood cocktail services and so on are dealt with in conjunction with recipes and general considerations of methods in the sections concerned.

CHAPTER 3

LIQUORS AND COMMODITIES

Just as a chef de cuisine must desirably have a knowledge and appreciation of the basic materials he uses, so the restaurateur or maître d'hôtel and members of his staff are likely to improve on their preparations at the guéridon the more they study the commodities they employ. Even in the case of "standard" dishes that are flambé-d or guéridon cooked there are possibilities for individuality according to the establishment. It is, indeed, important that restaurateurs not only study the nature of the commodities they use but also keep fully abreast of the range of home produced and imported foodstuffs and liquors available.

SPIRITS AND LIQUEURS FOR FLAMBÉ

As it is the alcohol or spirit that takes the flame it is apparent that higher proof spirits (70% and upwards) are the most suitable for flambé dishes. Milder liqueurs may, especially in sweet dishes, be used to impart flavour, but for final flaring the choice desirably falls on a high proof spirit usually cognac (or similar distillations such as armagnac or the marcs of wine), rum and whisky though, of course, other spirits such as vodka or aquavit may be used.

When using wine and spirits generally in food and cookery it is sometimes overlooked that almost all the alcohol is evaporated or burnt in such usage. The culinary intention in adding such liquors is most often to give flavour and character to a dish and, additionally, in the case of flambé work, a touch of spectacle. Flavour rather than alcohol content is important in cooking; both are important in flambé-ing. In good cookery, whether conducted in cuisine or restaurant, the idea of using "cooking sherry" or inferior quality wines and spirits for culinary use should be entirely alien. Wine and spirits in food and in cooking food should be as high in quality and flavour as those chosen to accompany food as a beverage. Because taste counts, it is important to select the best quality and the best flavoured wines and liqueurs for flambé and culinary use generally as is possible.

In the U.S.A. and possibly elsewhere high alcohol content liquors incorporating flavours, such as grape and other fruit brandies, are marketed specifically for flambé work. Branded flambé liquors of this kind may, because of their high alcohol content, be efficient and effective for ignition and flaming. The perfectionist maître d'hôtel will, doubtless, still prefer to use those brandies and liqueurs which he knows by experience to be able to stand additionally the flavour test. This is not mere conservatism.

Blending for Flavour

A very wide range, indeed, of spirits and liqueurs are capable of being flamed, even those of relatively low alcohol content, providing they are used with skill and also in the warm. Obviously, however, it is the "straighter" spirits such as brandy, whisky, rum, gin, vodka, the various forms of aquavit which, because of their readiness to flame, are chiefly used. The recipe examples in this manual serve to give an idea of the types of dishes for which the different liquors are appropriate and clearly some flamable liquors, because of their flavour (or lack of it) will tend to have much more limited use than, say, brandy which forms an acceptable blend with a wide range of sweet and savoury foods, or rum which has a good range in sweet cookery. Many experimentalists, however, are finding how effectively Scotch whisky may be used in flambé work and even gin can make a good dish especially if the gin flavour is further brought out by the use of additional juniper berries in the flavouring.

In using liqueurs which incorporate spice, herb and fruit flavourings, alcohol content or strength will possibly determine the degree to which they are employed for the actual flaming as distinct from their addition in earlier stages for flavouring and blending. Thus in versions of crêpe Suzette the orange flavoured liqueurs, whilst an important component, are nearly always supplemented by cognac for the final flaring.

It is again stressed that the recipes in this manual may be regarded as examples and as pointers to formulae rather than being an attempt to chart all flambé possibilities. Such dishes give great opportunity for further and infinite blends but in so doing it may be helpful to have in mind some general considerations to avoid abortive trials. For example, some of the softer or sweeter liqueurs can result in unpleasantly cloying sauces when used for crêpe work or in similar sweet dishes and the success of crêpe Suzette undoubtedly hinges on the introduction of the more tart flavour of orange and the touch of lemon. Possibilities do exist for crêpe dishes with, for example, Drambuie, but the honey-like background again needs the introduction of piquancy if sickliness is to be avoided.

On the other hand some spirits such as vodka and the other forms of aquavit leave virtually no residual flavour. These invariably require relatively strong reinforcement by flavoursome liquors at an earlier stage. Blending sauce both sweet and savoury may be an adventurous and highly experimental process in this field as in other culinary ones but success is seldom achieved by flouting basic, gastronomic principles.

The following short list of possible liquors is provided as an aide memoire for those experimenting with or attempting to compose guéridon or flambé dishes.

SHORT LIST OF LIQUORS FOR FLAMBÉ

Liqueurs

The following are sweet or sweetish. Most will flame under favourable conditions but, in general, less readily than those listed under spirits.

Name	Predominant flavour or characteristic
Abricota	Apricot
Abricotine	Apricot
Advocaat	Brandy and eggs
Amourette	Colour of violets, vanilla type flavour
Ananas, crème d'	Pineapple
Anisette	Aniseed
Angelica	Yellow, spicy liqueur
Apry	Apricot

Name	*Predominant flavour or characteristic*
Athol Brose	Oatmeal, whisky and, possibly, egg
Aurum (Italian)	Golden colour, aromatic
Banane, crème de	Banana
Barat Palinka (Hungarian)	Apricot
Benedictine	Aromatic herby compound
Brontë	A British liqueur
Cacao, crème de	Chocolate or cocoa and vanilla
Capricot	Apricot
Cassis, crème de	Blackcurrant
Chartreuse	Two types; green (stronger) and yellow, pungent and spicy
Cherry brandy	Cherries
Cointreau	Orange. (A brand of curaçao)
Cordial Médoc	Distilled wine, spicy
Cumin, crème de	Cumin seed
Curaçao	Orange
Drambuie	Scotch whisky, heather honey
Forbidden Fruit	Grapefruit (U.S.A.)
Fraises, crème de	Strawberry
Framboise, crème de	Raspberries
Glayva	Scotch whisky base
Glen Mist	Scotch whisky base
Grand Marnier	Orange (a brand of curaçao)
Irish coffee liqueur	Irish made liqueur
Irish Mist	Irish liqueur
Kirseboer liqueur	Danish Cherry brandy
Kahlua	Coffee flavoured liqueur
Kummel	Caraway and cumin
Lindisfarne	Made on the Holy Island of Lindisfarne, Northumberland, from Scotch, honey and local herbs
Mandarine	Tangerines
Maraschino	Cherries
Menthe, crème de	White or green in colour, mint
Moka, crème de	Coffee
Morella Cherry Brandy	English made by Grants
Noyau, crème de	Fruit kernels (cherries)
Parfait Amour	Violets and vanilla

Name	*Predominant flavour or characteristic*
Peach brandy	Peaches
Prunelle	Plums
Rose, crème de	Rose aroma
Strega	Italian, orange flavoured liqueur
Tia Maria	Jamaican coffee liqueur
Usquebaugh	Old form name for whisky
Van der Hum	South African, tangerine fruit
Vanille, crème de	Vanilla
Violette, crème de	Violets
Vieille Curé	Aromatic, spicy
Yvette, crème	U.S.A. made violet coloured

Spirits

The following will flame readily under reasonable conditions, though it is not suggested that they are all likely to enhance dishes.

Name	
Akvavit (Scandinavian)	Rectified spirit, usually caraway flavoured
Aquavit	Spirit
Aquavitae	Italian form of brandy
Armagnac	Brandy (less esteemed than cognac)
Bacardi	A Puerto Rican rum, light colour
Bourbon	U.S.A. fermented grain (predominantly maize) mash whisky
Brandy	Distilled wine
Bushmills whiskey	Best known N. Ireland whiskey
Cognac	Brandy from the more esteemed brandy region of France
Daiquiri	A Puerto Rican rum
Eau-de-vie	French form of aquavit or spirit (i.e. eau-de-vie de vin, brandy)
Fine champagne	Brandy, correctly either a Petite Champagne or Grande Champagne
Fine maison	The brandy "of the house", the selected brandy of the establishment

Geneva	Hollands gin
Gin	London Gin, dry; Plymouth Gin, sweeter
Grappa	Italian spirit distilled from grape residue
Goldwasser	Flavoured spirit garnished with fragments of gold leaf
Hollands	Dutch gin (juniper flavoured)
Irish whiskey	Grain (predominantly barley), pot-stilled whiskey
Kirsch	Distilled from cherries, colourless
Marc	Spirit from residue from grapes (after wine making) or apples (after cider making)
Mirabelle	Plum spirit (sometimes sweetened)
Quetsch	Plum brandy
Rum	Distilled from molasses
Rye	Rye grain whisky
Schiedam	Hollands gin
Scotch whisky	May be "single malt", pot-stilled from malted mashed fermented barley or blended, i.e. mixed with grain spirit
Slivovitz	Polish plum spirit
Tequila	Harsh Mexican spirit distilled from fermented sap
Vodka	Spirit

Further Liquors

Strong aperitifs such as pastis like Pernod, Ricard and the Greek Ouzo may also be used for flambé work.

Bitters

The following may be considered for flavouring.

Abbots Aged Bitters (U.S.A.)	Fernet Branca (Italy)
Angostura (Trinidad)	Orange Bitters
Amer Picon (France)	Peach Bitters
Campari (Italy)	Sécrestat (France)

WINES IN GUÉRIDON COOKERY

The way in which wine is used generally in professional cookery is well known. Because the processes involved in cookery at the table are preferably short ones the use of wine, whilst remaining desirable, is necessarily conditioned and to some extent restricted by such considerations.

Fortified Wines

It is, therefore, only natural that the emphasis tends to be on the fortified wines, that is those which have been strengthened during their making by the addition of spirit (normally brandy). Fortified wines are particularly useful in guéridon dishes because, generally speaking, they either require less reduction to communicate their flavour and bouquet adequately or, alternatively, because of their higher alcoholic content are, in any case, capable of more rapid reduction.

For cooking at the side table, therefore, the principal fortified wines used for aperitifs or dessert wines merit particular attention. Notes in the recipe section are indicative of typical use but here attention may properly be drawn to the fact that whilst recipes may show typical usage, the individuality and flair of the operator can be brought to bear on such use. For instance, substitution of one wine for another may often yield both interesting and satisfactory results.

The following wines must especially be borne in mind for table cookery; sherries, Madeira, Marsala, port. These names indicate, of course, a wide range of types and it is clear that vastly different flavours and results will be achieved when, for example, a sherry of dry, light fino type is used as against a rich Oloroso. Probably in cooking the richer and more fully flavoured wines may tend to suggest themselves first but the cook at table need take nothing for granted. He can and should attempt to train his palate to guide his cookery in using wines in an interesting way.

Whilst fortified wines can, when carefully handled, be used to achieve a flambé effect (note for example the recipes for flambé-d consommé in Chapter 5) their use in this way is unusual. It is probably too tricky a procedure to commend itself as wholly practicable during the hurly-burly of a busy restaurant service. As in the case of spirits and liqueurs, place emphasis on quality and flavour. The idea of low-grade cooking wine should gain no support in professional circles.

Also capable of classification amongst fortified wines are some of the French and Italian aperitif wines bearing brand names, and also, of course, the various types of vermouth. The French aperitifs, broadly speaking, tend to be sweet and thus are probably best exploited in the making of sweet items. The vermouths may, however, be introduced into a wider variety of savoury as well as sweet items. Some appropriate use, for example, is in table-cooked savoury dishes using veal and chicken.

Table Wines

The enormous range of white, red and rosé wines play an important role in professional cookery. It is within the kitchen itself that they are used to maximum and best effect for in so many instances wines are best blended with reductions of fumets or sauces and themselves must be reduced or take their part in the reduction.

On the other hand, there remains scope for imaginative use of table wine at the guéridon not only in dishes requiring heat and actual cooking but also in the macerating of fruits and in the general preparation of cold sweets. The maître d'hôtel and other restaurant staff might, with benefit, study many of the classic, basic uses of wine in behind the scenes cookery with a view to adaptations for swifter preparations "in the room".

An example of a promotional use of wine for presentation is in the mounting of a cleaned, half bottle or miniature bottle of champagne within a mound of hot choucroûte or sauerkraut so that on presentation the wine flows out over the contents of the dish.

COMMODITIES AT THE GUÉRIDON

Manufactured Sauces

Many restaurateurs and gourmets alike believe that manufactured, bottled sauces, pickles and other relishes are abused rather than used by British diners. Similarly, an over-addiction to tomato ketchup characterises many American eaters. Gourmet restaurants and, indeed, establishments with any pretensions to high quality cooking and service are likely to limit strictly their use of pre-prepared, manufactured accompaniments of this kind. They may rightly feel that it is hardly an advertisement for the dishes of the house should bottled preparations be widely displayed on sideboard and guéridon.

There are, nevertheless, occasions when some manufactured sauces and preparations may be brought into restaurant use. Certainly whilst dedicated restaurateurs should seek to guide and educate the taste of the public they serve, they must in the overwhelming number of cases be equally ready to meet their customers' demands.

It is neither possible, desirable nor necessary to consider each and every type of manufactured sauce or pickle, but the following points may be of assistance in determining the use of such aids, particularly in the preparation of guéridon dishes.

Worcestershire Sauce

The precise formula for Worcestershire sauce is one which manufacturers seek to guard but basically this thin liquor, which is not cooked, results from macerating a blend of spices and fruit in vinegar and soy base, allowing time for maturity in the cask. Indeed, though differing in flavour there is some affinity between Worcestershire sauce and soy sauce.

Conventionally offered with certain dishes such as tomato juice and Scotch broth, waiters also use Worcestershire sauce for flavouring many lamp meat dishes such as Monkey Gland Steak and Steak Diane. They also use it when blending seafood cocktail sauces and even salad dressings. As the sauce has a distinctive taste and colour its use in this way as an ingredient should be much more restricted than it commonly is. Limited to one or two specialities a dash of Worcestershire sauce may give a permissible touch of interest. It should not be regarded as an unfailing support for all preparations. Both in serving and using the sauce, it may be noted that if used without shaking the clearer fluid at the top (with sediment still resting at the bottom) the sauce is both milder and clearer. It may be preferred for some purposes used in this unshaken form.

Tobasco

Another "non-cooked" relish is Tobasco, which has been described by its manufacturers as "the red pepper seasoning which is matured like fine wine". Originated in Louisiana, U.S.A., it is a strong and pungent liquor and has long been used by maîtres d'hôtel in tomato cocktails, seafood cocktails and, of course, as an accompaniment for oysters, clams and other seafoods. It can be incorporated in cooked dishes needing "bite".

Ketchups

Tomato ketchup, despite its popularity with Americans and many British eaters, should not be necessary, as a general rule, as an addition to properly cooked, garnished and dressed food. Like many other bottled preparations, however, it can effect a "rescue operation" for really dull fare. Waiters do use it to blend dressings and clearly tomato ketchup is an item which cannot be denied to guests who may find it agreeable in seafood cocktail sauces and so on.

Mushroom ketchup either prepared in the kitchens or purchased ready manufactured (though it is now something of a rarity) is a useful aid in guéridon work and would certainly help to relieve the reliance of unimaginative waiters on Worcestershire sauce. Chinese manufactured mushroom sauce may be considered as a substitute for traditional English mushroom ketchup.

Chutneys and Oriental Condiments

Sweet mango chutney (including its spicier sub-divisions such as Colonel Skinner and Major Grey) is not only what British diners conventionally demand with curry but may also usefully, when chopped, help to spice and flavour guéridon preparations. There is considerable variation in strength and spiciness between brands and blends and, as in the case of mustard, sampling and choice is necessary.

Apart from chutneys, however, there are many prepared Indian condiments such as lime, brinjal, prawn and papaya pickle and hot mango kasundi. These should be considered for giving a touch of interest to guéridon meat dishes.

Similar thought may be given not only to chili and soy sauce from the range of Chinese preparations but also to their oyster sauce and to Chinese mixed pickles.

Pickles

Chopped pickles, such as gherkins or dill cucumbers or pickled walnuts, have uses in cold compounds and also for some hot dishes.

Mixed pickles and piccalili may also, when chopped, be introduced with discretion into some dressings. Strong raw flavours of this kind are, however, seldom the choice of gourmets.

Mustards

Mustards are also considered in the section on salads and salad dressings. Suffice it to indicate at this stage that a wide variety of strengths and flavours may be obtained in French mustards. Even amongst restaurant staff it is a common misconception that French mustard must be a dark coloured, sweetish preparation lacking bite. Care should be taken in sampling brands and blends so as to achieve consistent preparations in making guéridon dishes.

Salt and Peppers

It has become obvious in recent years how restaurant clients whether they be simple or sophisticated respond to the presentation of their condiments. For example, French mustards in the attractive china containers and peppers from the moulin or mill have universal appeal.

Gros sel which should, in any case, correctly be presented with dishes such as boiled beef is nowadays more widely used because of the obvious pleasure taken by guests in grinding gros sel through the small, wooden container or in seeing this done by the waiter at the guéridon. It is doubtful whether there is any great gain in flavour by the use of gros sel but there can be little doubt that the use of gros sel grinders and pepper mills at the guéridon has much to commend it for promotional reasons alone.

Peppers, with mustards and other condiments, are more fully considered in the section on salads and salad dressings where their use is of particular importance.

Vinegar

Further consideration is also given to vinegar in the salad and salad dression section. At this juncture it is re-emphasised that if one were pedantic one would deny the word vinegar to the malt preparations which should more accurately be described as alegar except that this word has fallen into disuse. The more ordinary forms of malt vinegar are really of little use for high class restaurant work and considerable care should be taken in selecting good quality wine vinegar both red and white. Cider vinegar is also obtainable but has dubious merit as a condiment for guéridon use. All vinegars are capable of taking flavouring, particularly garlic and tarragon, and to buy vinegars pre-flavoured by having the herbs or spices steeped in them or doing this in advance for the restaurant is a useful preliminary step in mise en place.

FLAVOURINGS FOR SWEET DISHES

Apart from the flavourings given by liqueurs, there is a range of commodities which should be considered both as garnishes and flavourings for sweet dishes. These need not be confined to the blending of sauces prepared in the blazer but for garnishing the interior of crêpes or scattering on fruits that have been flared. These include:

Candied, Crystallised and Preserved Fruits

Effective use may be made of preserved fruits of all kinds including Chinese preserved ginger, lotus nuts in syrup, cumquats and chow chow. Sliced ginger blended with whipped cream can make an effective crêpe filling.

Simpler candied fruits, grated or chopped, can also be used in such dishes.

Syrups

Manufactured syrups such as those flavoured with grenadine, cassis or mint may be found of some use in preparing sweet dishes.

Indian perfumed waters and Gulkand of roses (rose petal jam) may also be exploited. Greek, Scotch and other honeys may suggest applications.

Nuts

Toasted, slivered almonds, blanched almonds, whole and chopped walnuts, pistachios, cashews and other types may be considered for garnishing and blending and also, of course, nuts incorporated into praliné.

Sugar

An important commodity for the sweet items of guéridon and flambé work, the choice and service of table sugar present little difficulty. Obviously, the finer caster sugar is the common choice

for most guéridon purposes. It is, perhaps, worth bearing in mind'
however, that sugar may be more subtly flavoured by being stored
with vanilla pods and even other spices such as cinnamon stick.
For some dishes sugar blended with cinnamon or other powdered
spice can be convenient. Brown sugars, Demerara, sand sugar,
Barbados sugars, obviously suggest themselves for dishes to be
flamed with rum.

Manufactured Sweet Sauces

These have little or no use in large operations but small proprietors
may find it a convenience (though probably a costly one) to have
manufactured sweet sauces as reserve mise en place. Small operators have even made imaginative use of manufactured fruit purées
in can or bottle as a short cut to achieving the basis for some sauces
for table use.

Flavouring Possibilities

The foregoing notes have been provided as a means of indicating
the types of liquors and commodities to be considered for guéridon and flambé work and some of the more important principles
concerning their use and selection. It is also hoped that they will
indicate the infinite range rather than chart narrow possibilities.
Those who aspire to develop attractive guéridon cookery may be
stimulated to further investigation and study of the materials that
may be used and blended for this style of work.

CHAPTER 4

DISHES FOR GUÉRIDON PREPARATION

During the years that service in the restaurant has been developed there has been a natural evolution of dishes which have lent themselves particularly to exploitation from the guéridon. It will already be apparent from the preliminary chapters that virtually all food may be served from the side table or guéridon and that, indeed, in many types of restaurant operation all items are dispensed to the guest in this way. Bearing in mind that flambé (and similar specialities) are the subject of separate chapters as are other speciality aspects such as dressing a salad and presentation, the object of this section is not to consider *all* the foods which can conceivably be prepared or completed at the side table but rather a selection of those types of items which are either traditionally so served or which by their nature are especially suited for this treatment.

Preparation Principles

One or two basic principles touched upon elsewhere must be re-emphasised in considering dishes suitable either for cookery or completion at the guéridon. Of these, of paramount importance is that the cooking or completion can be accomplished within a reasonably short period of time. Quite apart from the question of the high cost of skilled labour and the impracticability of keeping skilled operators for unduly long periods of time on guéridon cookery or finishing there is, of course, the important aspect of tedium for the guest and the prolongation and concentration of culinary odours.

Thus the most important guéridon dishes tend to be found amongst the following groups:

1. Appetisers such as cold soups, fruit appetisers, seafood and similar cocktails which mostly involve simple assembly of prepared ingredients (salads involve similar considerations).
2. Pastas (Italian pastes) and noodles which demand merely the finishing touches of saucing and garnishing to previously though freshly cooked pâtes.
3. Such meat, poultry, game or fish dishes as are capable of extremely rapid cookery.
4. Sweets which are capable of quick cookery or, alternatively, those in which cold and pre-prepared items are blended together.

Recipes and suggestions are, therefore, in this section grouped into those categories.

SALADE D'ORANGE—ORANGE SALAD

Mise en place: Oranges (two per portion), caster sugar, kirsch (if desired), sharp knife, service spoon and two forks, timbale (or glass bowl or entrée dish), 8-oz. goblets, underplates with d'oyleys, sundae spoons, napkin, two saucers (one with water, one with sugar).

Method:

1. Arrange the mise en place neatly and in sequence on the side table.
2. Using knife and fork, slice a cap of skin and pith from the stem end of the orange.
3. Push the fork through this skin and pith (the zest—outer skin of orange—towards the handle) so that it forms a hilt or guard.
4. With the guarded fork, impale the orange and holding it up remove the remaining skin with a sharp knife and in one continuous strip.
5. Now fillet the orange, allowing each sliver to fall into the timbale or entrée dish.
6. Extract all juice by squeezing the pithy core or skeleton

between spoon and fork (some use two plates for this operation).

7. Repeat with the other oranges as required.

8. Sweeten as necessary or desired with caster sugar and remove any pips whilst stirring to blend in sugar.

9. If required or desired flavour with the kirsch (or even another liqueur).

10. Decorate and dress the goblets by dipping rim in water then in saucer of sugar.

11. Fill the goblets with orange slivers and divide the juice equally amongst the goblets.

12. Place goblets on d'oyley-covered small underplates, flank with sundae spoon and serve.

There are alternative modes of peeling an orange before the guest. A simpler one is: Using a knife and fork and working on a plate, remove a "cap" from the top and bottom of the orange. With the orange held firm on one of these flattened ends and secured with the fork, cut away the peel in downward slices following the curve of the orange.

Grapefruit and Florida Cocktails

Grapefruit, ugli fruit, oranges and other citrous fruit cocktails can be given emphasis by similar guéridon preparation. Such cocktails may be completed by flavouring with kirsch, curaçao, maraschino or other liqueurs. Single fruits or blends of fruit may be compounded in this way. Florida Cocktail normally includes grapefruit and orange topped with a cherry.

Pineapples, Melons and other Fruits

Many tart or refreshing fruits may be guéridon prepared and flavoured with liqueurs, wine and spirit for appetiser use.

In the following examples of melon, it can be left to discretion which preliminary stages (e.g. scooping out) may be left for "behind the scenes".

MELON DE CHARENTE AUX LIQUEURS

Nowadays small cantaloup melons are as likely to come from Israel as from Charente but whether they are "veritable Charentais" or not they make effective presentation.

Slice the top from the melon to form a cup and scoop out the

seeds with a stainless spoon. Blend the chosen liqueur or spirit with
two tablespoons caster sugar and pour into the cavity. Allow to
chill thoroughly and to macerate for at least 2 hours. Serve on a
bed of crushed ice.

CANTALOUP AU PORTO

Similarly top off a cap from a cantaloup melon. Scoop out the
seeds and, using a parisienne spoon, scoop out the flesh. Macerate
the little balls of melon in caster sugar (about 2 oz.) and a glass of
white port and replace within the melon case. Present the melon
case bedded on ice and serve into glass goblets or fruit cocktail
coupes at the side table. If using glass goblets, decorate by dipping
in egg white and then in sugar, plain or tinted with sap green or
diluted cochineal for example.

When small Charentais melons are used, they may be halved for
similar scooping out and macerating treatment and then presented
and served direct to the guest in the half case in a large coupe.

Various wines and liqueurs together with orange and lemon
juice may be used for blends for melon and melon cocktails.

Mario Gallati at London's famous Caprice has shown how individuality and novelty can have gastronomic appeal in his appetiser
Coupe Caprice which combines diced melon and prawns, blended
with mayonnaise, cream and ketchup and flavoured further with
green and red peppers, tarragon, Tobasco sauce and seasoning.
This is served chilled in coupes.

Avocado

Avocado pears though most often prepared in the kitchen are
capable of guéridon completion or even preparation *ab initio*. They
require merely halving and removal of stone. The flesh in the
halved avocado may be scored with a knife to facilitate the penetration of vinaigrette or other dressing. For filling the cavity and
for dressing the diced avocado flesh, seafood and other cocktail
mixes may be considered, and also the vinaigrettes and dressings
listed in the salad chapter.

SOUPS

Cold Soups

Some cold soups such as wine soup and fruit soups are possibilities for guéridon assembling and completion. Vichysoisse and

adaptations of it can also be completed with cream and chopped chives at the side table.

Cold bortsch made by blending chilled regular bortsch with yoghourt (or sour cream) and lemon juice may also be considered as worth exploitation.

In the following example for cold Spanish soup quantities need not be followed as it is thought the executant should find his own precise formula and then adhere to it. There are many variants.

GAZPACHO

1 teasp. chopped chives	1 demi-tasse olive oil
½ teasp. chopped parsley	⅓ demi-tasse lemon juice and/or
½ teasp. chopped chervil	vinegar
1 dessertsp. chopped pimento	1 breakfastcup diced cucumber
½ sliced Spanish onion	(or sliced)
1 clove crushed garlic	Seasoning
2 large tomatoes concassés	Ice water as necessary

Method:

1. In a glass or china bowl over crushed ice, pound the chopped chives, chervil and parsley with the crushed, chopped garlic, pepper from the mill and salt.

2. Add a little iced water, pimento, diced cucumber and the tomato concassé.

3. Beat in the oil slowly and flavour with lemon (and/or vinegar). Adjust the consistency with iced water.

4. Garnish with sliced Spanish onions and cucumber and complete the seasoning. (This may be added to individual servings) and serve in chilled soup bowls or soup plates.

Accompaniments: Sauceboat of white breadcrumbs or trimmed pieces of white bread.

This Spanish cold soup, a speciality of Andalusia, may provide inspiration for sophisticated adaptations for an individualistic cold "soup of the house". This despite Theophile Gautier's uncomplimentary remarks about it following his Spanish journeyings in the early half of the nineteenth century. He called it a "hell broth".

Hot Soups
Several soups, because of their customary accompaniments or style
of service, for example Petite Marmite, Bortsch and Minestrone,
lend themselves to guéridon service. Few soups are actually completed at the side table but one which may be is:

POTAGE GERMINY

1 oz. chiffonade of sorrel	1 tablesp. cream
½ pint strong, white chicken	3 oz. butter
stock or white consommé	Chervil leaf tips
2 egg yolks	

Escoffier's manner of making *Potage Germiny* which is now a
culinary classic can hardly be improved; though one may doubt
whether the great maître chef would approve of its being done
outside the kitchen. It is, however, a soup that lends itself to preparation at the side table and, what is more, is suggestive of variants using liquors other than white consommé and adding varied
garnishes on completion. It is made as follows:

Method:
    1. Keeping the consommé hot, sweat the shredded sorrel
in about one-third of the butter.
    2. Add the consommé and bring to near boiling point.
    3. Blend the egg yolks with the cream and stirring con-
stantly pour this egg yolk and cream liaison into the consommé with the flame turned low beneath. Continue to heat
but do not allow to boil.
    4. With the flame almost extinguished and to ensure that
the mix does not boil, finish by dropping in the remaining
butter in small pieces, stirring constantly.
    5. When serving garnish with a pinch of chervil leaf
tips.

EXTRAIT DE BŒUF À LA CRÈME
Few duck presses are in full daily use. On days when *canard à la
presse* is not a *plat du jour* a rather costly soup may be made as
follows:

Have ready:

1 underdone rump steak (even topside beef will do)
¼ pint strong beef consommé or petite marmite
2 tablesp. cream
1 teasp. glace de viande
1 dessertsp. sherry
Salt, pepper

To prepare:

    1. Cut the warm, freshly grilled steak into walnut size pieces.

    2. Squeeze through the press using a little hot consommé to ensure maximum extraction.

    3. Heat over the lamp adding any remaining consommé and stirring in the glace de viande (meat glaze).

    4. Stir in the cream (do not allow the mix to boil), then the sherry and adjust the seasoning.

For the frail, exotic and wealthy, a final garnish of two raw oysters may be plopped in.

SEAFOOD COCKTAILS

Seafood Cocktail Sauces

Filippo Ferrari, the celebrated restaurateur whose chief years of fame were at the Berkeley revealed in his memoires, *From Candle Light to Flash Light*, not only how popular his Marie Rose cocktail sauce had been with diners, sophisticated and simple alike, but incidentally how fundamentally simple it was. Yet Ferrari's flavouring of a basic mayonnaise with items such as Worcestershire sauce, piccalilli juice, tomato ketchup, squeeze of lemon and cream (even in wartime, from the top of the milk bottle) is basically the way in which all maîtres d'hôtel approach this task.

George Rector of the famous Rector's Restaurant of New York prepared shell fish cocktails with a sauce which was stronger stuff than Ferrari's for basically it was three parts tomato ketchup to one part grated horseradish thinned with lemon juice, Worcestershire sauce and with a seasoning of tobasco and salt. Such blends, even of the "masters", sometimes make poor reading but with the sales force of personality and enough stylishness of presentation some of these mixes which seem to have in almost everything from

Preparing Oranges for Salad or Cocktail

1. In preparing citrus fruits in the room contact of the hands with the fruit must be avoided. The picture shows how the first slice of peel and pith from the orange top is slid on to the fork to act as a guard to prevent the fingers touching the orange to be peeled. Notice that the peel is then removed in one continuous strip; thus a well sharpened knife is essential. The blend of grapefruit and orange in the cocktail may be completed with a liqueur at choice.

2. Once the peel has been removed, the waiter cuts out segments of orange flesh leaving behind the pith and connecting tissue. Note the double cocktail coupe in the foreground of which the inner container is ice filled. An alternative service is a sugar rimmed goblet in the rear.

Seafood Cocktail

In this case the cocktail is of prawns (cocktail de crevettes roses). The peeled prawns have been blended with cocktail sauce and are then spooned into coupes—either the ice-lined double coupe in hotel plate in the foreground or the parsley rimmed goblet as an alternative. Partially peeled prawns balanced on the rim complete the décor.

nearby bottles can achieve success. The following seafood cocktail sauces are given merely as a basis for experimentation and adaptation.

SEAFOOD COCKTAIL SAUCE, MAYONNAISE BASED

¼ pint mayonnaise   1 tablesp. tomato concassé
Teasp. or squeeze lemon juice   1 dessertsp. cream
Dash of Worcestershire sauce   1 dessertsp. tomato ketchup

Note: Other mayonnaise derivatives such as Remoulade sauce thinned with a little cream may be used to prepare, for example, Shrimp Remoulade in cocktail style.

SEAFOOD COCKTAIL SAUCE, TOMATO BASED

¼ pint tomato concassé   Squeeze lemon juice
2 tablesp. tomato ketchup   1 dessertsp. chili sauce
1 teasp. horseradish   1 level dessertsp. sugar
Dash of Tobasco

Such a basic mix may also be blended with sour or fresh cream. Whilst maîtres d'hôtel and waiters may be encouraged to devise their own cocktail sauces, they should aim at a consistent formula. At the same time it may be stressed that one of the features of restaurant blends, as distinct from kitchen recipes, is that the restaurateur may adjust his mixes to meet the individually known tastes, or what is judged to be the likely tastes of his clients.

Generally speaking, Americans accustomed to palate-anaesthetising iced and strong aperitif drinks, relish rather strong peppery blends, whilst European taste tends to favour milder mixes based on mayonnaise or cream.

For service of seafood cocktails use double coupes (with ice liner) or wine goblets.

COCKTAIL DE CREVETTES ROSES—PRAWN COCKTAIL

Mise en place:

Peeled prawns   Concassé tomato
Mayonnaise   Tomato ketchup
Sieved egg, yolk and   Cayenne pepper, paprika pepper
    white   Salt

1. Lightly dress shredded lettuce with vinaigrette (recipes given in Chapter 9) and place a little in each individual coupe or glass.

2. Place on a teaspoonful of concassé tomato.

3. Blend a dressing of mayonnaise flavoured with tomato ketchup and cayenne pepper (or any adaptation of seafood cocktail sauces).

4. Add the cleaned, peeled prawns to the dressing and spoon the mixture into the lettuce and tomato based coupes.

5. Sprinkle with sieved egg and/or paprika and place cleaned but unpeeled prawn on the coup or goblet rim and/or a half lemon sliver, slit to fit.

Serve seafood cocktails whether in goblets or double coupes on an underplate (preferably d'oyley dressed) with coupe or cocktail spoon on the right and oyster fork on the left.

SHRIMP COCKTAIL

Similarly prepared and garnished but cocktail sauce and décor varied at choice.

LOBSTER COCKTAIL

Also assembled in similar style, the basic mise en place includes: diced or sliced lobster meat, sliced hard boiled egg, chopped tarragon and parsley, shredded lettuce, tomato concassé, a seafood cocktail sauce at choice.

BISMARCK COCKTAIL

Mis en place:

Boned rollmop herrings	Diced celery
Vinaigrette dressing	Shredded lettuce
Diced cucumber	Tobasco or chili sauce
Paprika or capers	

For this economical seafood cocktail for more modest restaurant operations:

1. Ensure the herring is free of skin and bone; then cut into dice or strips.

2. Combine the cut herring with shredded lettuce, diced cucumber and celery.

3. Dress lightly with vinaigrette dressing flavoured to taste with tobasco or chili sauce.

4. Place into coupes or glasses, top with fanned out gherkins, chopped egg, capers and/or paprika.

The foregoing treatment of rollmops may suggest other economical possibilities using, for example, marinated cooked white fish with a light garnishing of chopped anchovies dressed and assembled as for seafood cocktails generally.

ITALIAN PASTES AND NOODLES

Of the Italian pastes and noodles, the most commonly served as a standard guéridon feature item in restaurants in Britain and U.S.A. is spaghetti. Italian restaurants in these countries are, however, likely to feature other pastas, particularly ribbon types such as fettucine and lasagne, including lasagne verde.

For guéridon service either the lamp and blazer may be used or preferably the older style chafing dish with deeper pan. The spaghetti (or other pastas) should previously be cooked in the kitchen "al dente" and, also in the kitchen, very lightly dressed with a little oil, butter or a mix of the two (leaving the remaining dressing to be completed at the guéridon). It will be clear that all of the customary sauces and dressings may be administered to the pasta from the guéridon. The following serves as an example:

SPAGHETTI NAPOLITAINE
Mise en place:

Butter   Tomato sauce   Grated parmesan cheese

Method:

1. Over moderate flame melt the butter in the chafing dish.

2. Add the cooked spaghetti, the warm tomato sauce and half the cheese.

3. Blend thoroughly by lifting the spaghetti with spoon and fork well clear of the pan and back again.

4. When thoroughly blended and hot, transfer to plates, similarly lifting the portions well clear of the pan.

5. Pass remainder of grated parmesan cheese separately.

Note: The cutlery required for these dishes is a large fork placed at the right of the guest's plate and a dessert spoon placed at the left of the plate. For correct service in the Italian style the plate should be a deep soup plate. The pepper mill should be included in the condiments made available on the table.

FETTUCINE ALFREDO

Mise en place:

Butter   Grated parmesan cheese

Method:

1. Melt a large nut of butter in the chafing dish.
2. Place in the strained, boiled fettucine.
3. Add further butter and grated parmesan cheese.
4. Combine together by lifting the pasta from the dish with spoon and fork.

Alfredo made his reputation in his small restaurant in Rome by the artistry with which, spotlighted, he performed this ritual with gold fork and spoon (given to him, so it was once rumoured, by admiring celebrities—was it Douglas Fairbanks and Mary Pickford?). The dish is simple and traditional but Alfredo's flair as a restaurateur-showman gave it distinction.

EGGS

Egg cooking in the domestic dining room at one time frequently involved the chafing dish. In restaurants, tying up the guéridon and the lamps by too much emphasis on minor dishes is not normally regarded as practical from a promotional point of view. Hence, egg dishes are not in modern times much featured on the lamp.

Clearly, however, the chafing dish is a good medium for preparing and presenting scrambled eggs in their best and freshest form. A touch of distinction can be given to such dishes by the addition of cream and by appropriate accompaniments such as, for example, asparagus tips, diced fonds d'artichaut, members of the mushroom family, truffles, tomato concassé, chipolatas, shrimps and prawns and diced ham.

CUISSES DE GRENOUILLES—FROGS' LEGS

Escoffier is credited with the poetic designation *Cuisses de nymphes* as an alternative for *Cuisses de grenouilles* so as not to offend the susceptibilities of Edward VII (though whilst that robust monarch possibly would appreciate the nymph allusions he seems an unlikely figure to jib at any delicate dish—even frogs). *Cuisses de nymphes* is now, certainly, an accepted menu description for frogs' legs.

Marinate the legs either in milk or in wine and aromates for an hour or so before use. Then drain, dry and dredge in lightly seasoned, sifted flour before sauter (or skewering then grilling).

For use in Britain, quick-frozen legs are obtainable which, on thawing, may be used as fresh ones.

Usually six legs are allowed per portion.

CUISSES DE NYMPHES AUX FINES HERBES

Frog's legs	Finely chopped shallot	Seasoning
Oil	Chopped parsley	Lemon
Butter		

Method:

1. Place a dessertspoonful of oil in the blazer over a moderate flame. Add butter. When hot add the chopped shallot.

2. Follow after half a minute, when the butter and oil is again hot, with the seasoned frogs' legs and sauter.

3. Toss frequently as the legs are inclined to "stick" to the pan and a palette knife is usually needed when this occurs.

4. Finish with lemon juice, further knob of butter and chopped parsley.

SHELL FISH DISHES

LOBSTER NEWBURG—I

1 boiled lobster (meat only, sliced)	1 gill cream
	2 oz. butter
½ glass sherry	3 egg yolks
½ glass cognac	Salt, pepper, nutmeg

Mise en place:

Have ready the lobster meat in slices and the egg yolks mixed with cream.

Method:

    1. Melt the butter, add the lobster and cook over moderate flame.

    2. After a minute or so, sprinkle with seasoning and add the wine then the brandy.

    3. Immediately follow by adding the liaison (the cream and egg yolk mix) stirring constantly.

    4. Continue to heat but do not allow to boil.

    5. When sauce thickens, serve immediately.

Other shell fish may similarly be prepared.

LOBSTER NEWBURG—2

Meat from 1 cooked lobster	1 oz. butter
2 egg yolks	1 teasp. chopped shallot
½ gill cream	Salt, paprika pepper
Nutmeg	

Garnish: Fleurons, sprigs of parsley.

Method:

    1. Melt the butter, add the chopped shallot and allow to cook without colouring over a steady flame.

    2. Add the lobster meat then the cream.

    3. When bubbling and hot reduce the flame and stir in the egg yolks. Do not allow to re-boil.

    4. Continuing to stir, season with salt and paprika (cayenne or tobasco if liked) and a little grated nutmeg.

    5. When thoroughly re-heated, serve with fleurons and garnish with sprigs of parsley.

SCAMPIS À LA CRÈME

½ pint cooked, peeled scampis	1 glass dry, light fino sherry
2 oz. sliced mushroom	1 gill cream
1 heaped teasp. chopped shallot	Juice of quarter lemon
	Salt, paprika and cayenne

Method:

    1. Acidulate the cream with lemon juice (alternatively, sour cream may be used).

    2. Melt the butter and, over steady flame, begin to sauter the shallot.

3. Just before the shallot begins to take colour add the mushrooms.

4. After a moment add the scampi and allow them to heat through thoroughly (at least 3 minutes).

5. Add the acidulated or sour cream, adjust the seasoning using salt (as necessary) and a dash of cayenne pepper and continue to heat.

6. Just before boiling point, finish by adding the sherry.

7. Serve lightly dusted with paprika.

Accompaniments: Rice (boiled or pilaff) or vol au vent or bouchée cases.

Variants: A little curry powder sauté-d with the shallots gives good flavour and might permit the designation, *Scampis à la crème Madras*.

MEAT AND POULTRY DISHES

STEAK TARTARE

This dish is supposed to reflect in a more sophisticated fashion the raw steak which, it is said, Tartar horsemen placed between the saddle and their mount's back to be pounded and crushed during a fierce ride. The modern version is commonly assembled and prepared from the guéridon.

Mise en place:

Minced or finely chopped raw fillet steak
Finely chopped raw onion and raw onion rings
Anchovy fillets, capers
Other flavourings to choice, e.g. Tabasco or Worcester sauce
Chopped hard boiled egg
Oil, vinegar
Salt, pepper (moulin and/or cayenne)
Raw egg

These ingredients should be chilled or very cold. Tartare steak is basically the pounded raw meat, dressed and shaped into a neat roundel with knife and fork or two forks. The dressing varies in emphasis according to the restaurateur's practice and, especially, in accordance with the guest's desire. Normally the minced steak is lightly dressed with oil, vinegar (in vinaigrette proportions and including a little Dijon mustard if desired), salt and pepper. If chopped onion is to be incorporated (it may be served separately as an accompaniment), it is first pressed on-to the plate with a knife blade before blending into the steak with the oil and vinegar. Some maîtres d'hôtel may also add chopped gherkin (similarly knife pressed) at this stage and also chopped anchovy fillet and capers. (Others may use anchovy fillets and capers as final garnish). Generally, further additions should be avoided unless asked for. The egg yolk (separated from the white) is dropped into a small well, made after shaping the steak. Some customers may like to blend their own yolk into the meat; some waiters blend in the egg to complete the dressing on the guéridon. Final decor may include onion rings, anchovy fillet in julienne strips, capers and chopped, hard boiled egg, yolk and white.

Oil and vinegar and other condiments are placed on the table and a salad is customary accompaniment.

Accompaniment: Thinly sliced black bread and butter (Danish rye or pumpernickel).

STEAK MINUTE AU POIVRE—PEPPERED MINUTE STEAK

Mise en place:

Fillet steak	Butter
Black pepper	Consommé (or good stock)
Oil	White wine

Method:

For steak au poivre when prepared in the kitchen thicker cuts, especially entrecôtes, may be used. For preparation "on the lamp" cuts from the fillet are recommended. In the kitchen (garde manger), flatten the steaks (with cutlet bat) introducing coarsely milled, black pepper so that the pepper particles firmly penetrate the meat. Use a moulin (pepper mill) or crush whole peppercorns with rolling pin.

In the room:

1. Ensure the minute steaks are adequately coated with pepper and then season with salt.

2. Melt the butter, add oil and when this mix is hot lay in the seasoned steaks.

3. Allow to brown well and quickly. Turn and brown reverse side.

4. Remove steaks to warm platter and keep hot.

5. Deglaze the pan with white wine and a little consommé over a high flame and when this has reduced to half add the cognac.

6. Adjust the seasoning of this sauce before pouring over the steak platter.

The steaks may be flamed with cognac if desired.

Accompaniments: Any variety of pommes frites, tossed green salad, grilled tomatoes and mushrooms.

FILET DE BŒUF STROGONOFF

2 large tomatoes, concassés	½ lb. beef fillet
1 dessertsp. mango chutney	2 tablesp. cream
2 oz. butter	1 tablesp. oil
1 shallot finely minced	Salt, pepper
1 tablesp. jus lié	

Method:

In the kitchen:

1. Prepare the beef by cutting into batons of one-inch lengths and of pencil thickness.

2. Prepare the concassé tomatoes by peeling, pipping and chopping.

3. Chop the mango chutney (Major Grey or Colonel Skinner are types recommended for tang) and finally chop the shallot.

In the room:

1. Heat the oil over steady flame and sauté the seasoned beef.

2. When the meat is well sealed, drain off the oil and add the butter and minced shallot and continue to cook.

3. Add the tomato concassé and a little jus lié.

4. When the shallot is softened, stir in the chopped chutney and cream and adjust the seasoning. Serve immediately.

Note: The distinctive touch of this version of Bœuf Strogonoff
has been attributed to Chef Meunier, chef de cuisine at the
Café de Paris in pre-war days and who was thought to have
worked in the kitchens of Tzarist Russia from where Strogonoff is said to have originated.

   As with so many guéridon dishes, Strogonoff has been adapted
by many individualists. A very common version is to use Worcestershire sauce for flavouring but this item tends to be overdone in
lamp cookery.

Accompaniments: Simply prepared vegetables such as new potatoes nature with green vegetables au beurre are good foils for
Bœuf Strogonoff and may be used as an alternative to the
somewhat inevitable rice. The cream used for Strogonoff is
usually considered better when sour or acidulated with a
squeeze of lemon.

VEAL ESCALOPE "BITTER SWEET"

1 escalope of veal
1 dessertsp. caster sugar
2 oz. butter
½ teasp. chopped julienne gherkins
Dash of wine vinegar or lemon juice
½ teasp. capers
Seasoning

Method:

   1. Heat the butter and sauter the escalope over moderately
hot flame.
   2. Put the veal to one side on a warm platter.
   3. Add the sugar and a further knob of butter to the pan
over a lowered flame and when foaming, add a dash of
vinegar (about a teaspoonful) or lemon juice (a little more)
and the gherkins and capers.
   4. When hot, replace the escalopes in this mix, heating and
turning them.

Accompaniments: pommes sautées, salad and/or green vegetables.

ESCALOPE DE VEAU EN PARAPLUIE—VEAL PARASOL

Mise en place:

Veal escalope, grated Parmesan, salt and pepper, butter, oil, lemon slices, olives, sauceboat of demi-glace.

In the larder:

1. Take a round escalope of veal about ½ to ¾ in. thick and cover with grated Parmesan cheese.

2. Flatten with a cutlet bat with pressing strokes from centre outwards so that the cheese adheres.

3. Continue to flatten, adding further cheese to both sides until the escalope is of minute steak thinness.

4. Season the cheese-impregnated escalope and then dip in beaten egg and white breadcrumbs.

In the room:

1. Over brisk flame, sauté the escalope in clarified butter to which a little oil has been added.

2. Allow both sides to colour.

3. Impale centre with cocktail stick or skewer topped with half a Spanish olive and serve with lemon slivers and a good demi-glace in separate sauceboat.

This dish is believed to have been developed in the Café de Paris around the turn of the century and was also exploited in Rectors in New York. Its name is derived, of course, from the umbrella effect of the edges curling on being beaten which becomes even more pronounced on cooking.

PICCATA AL MARSALA

Piccatas, small, rounded escalopes, are well suited for quick guéridon cookery. For a basic preparation with a marsala finished sauce:

1. Have a mise en place of small escalopes, dredged in sifted, seasoned flour, sauceboat of demi-glace or jus lié; butter and a little oil and a glass of marsala.

2. Heat the oil and butter and sauté the escalope.

3. When cooked and nicely coloured on each side, remove and keep warm. Strain off surplus butter and oil.

4. Deglaze the pan with jus lié. Add the marsala and finish with a few nuts of fresh butter, tossing the pan as they are added (monter au beurre).

TENDERLOIN OF PORK FLORIDA

1 lb. fillet of pork (2 × 8 oz. fillets)	Cos lettuce
	1 grapefruit
1 lemon	1 Jaffa orange
Paprika pepper	Butter
¼ sauceboat sauce piquante	Pepper from the mill

Method:

1. Cut the fillets lengthwise but not right through, so that they may be rolled flat to a thickness of about ¼ in. Dredge with seasoned flour.

2. Place butter in pan on table cooking stove at guéridon.

3. Add the pork and allow to cook.

4. While this is cooking, make salad dressing by squeezing lemon juice on to a plate and adding cream and shake of sugar.

5. Dress the salad with this and toss. Place sections of cos lettuce in half moons and orange and grapefruit sections on this. Place these on the table.

6. Pork should now be turned and allowed to cook until ready—approximately 2 minutes each side.

7. Place pork on two meat plates, add a measure of Madeira to the pan with about double the amount of sauce piquante which should then be dressed over the pork.

8. Serve and offer the vegetables.

Accompaniments: French fried potatoes and grilled tomatoes.

SUPRÊME DE VOLAILLE—FILLET OF CHICKEN

The breast with short trimmed wing bone attached and with the fillet lightly batted can readily be cooked at the guéridon. Basic method of preparing a *suprême de volaille à la crème* is as follows:

1. Heat a dessertspoonful of oil with a good knob of butter

and sauter the seasoned suprêmes. (They may be flour dredged if liked.)

2. When coloured and cooked through, put in the warm and pour away the surplus fat from the pan.

3. Deglaze the pan with good white, chicken consommé (strong, white chicken stock). Add the cream and finish with brandy or sherry.

4. Variants may be effected such as:

(a) Preliminary sauté-ing of spoonful of finely chopped shallot or onion.

(b) Varying the wine, spirit or liqueur flavouring.

(c) Using pre-prepared alternative sauces such as sauce allemande and also brown sauces.

(d) The introduction of garnish prior to finishing, e.g. strips of pimento, tomato concassé, mushrooms, cèpes and so on.

General Note on Veal, Pork, Chicken for Guéridon Dishes

In addition to the cooking of pork, chicken and veal as escalopes or piccata it is, of course, apparent that these meats may be pre-prepared, cut in batons, strips or in julienne for cooking in styles not dissimilar from sauté of Bœuf Strogonoff.

Such a basic approach permits the introduction of similarly cut garnish in varying proportions; for example, blends of such small batons as sauté-d pineapple tossed with sauté pork strips in the proportion of one part pineapple to four parts pork. Mushrooms, asparagus tips and similar garnishings may, of course, be blended with chicken and veal strips treated basically à la crème. For brown savoury versions tomato concassé, mushrooms, truffles, sauté-d shallots and onions may form the basis of blends.

OFFAL

ROGNONS À LA MINUTE

4 sheep's kidneys	1 glass Madeira
1 shallot	Soy sauce
4 medium mushrooms	2 croûtons
2 oz. butter	

In the kitchen:

1. Trim the kidneys of membrane, fat and gristle. Cut into fine slices and lightly dredge with sifted flour, seasoned with salt and pepper.

2. Finely chop the shallot and slice the mushrooms. (Cultivated mushrooms need not be peeled, but set aside the stalks for other culinary use such as duxelle.)

In the room:

1. Heat the butter and gently fry the chopped shallot.

2. Before the shallot colours, drop in the kidney and mushroom slices, turning up the flame so that they seal and sauté quickly.

3. After one minute, moisten with a glass of Madeira, add a dash of soy sauce and adjust salt and pepper seasoning.

4. Serve immediately, garnished with heart-shaped croûtons of butter-fried bread.

Note: *Kidneys à la minute* are capable of infinite variation for it is clear that sherry or Marsala may be used as alternatives to Madeira and even other wines or liqueurs may be substituted. Pig and veal kidneys may also be given similar treatment.

Liver and Other Offal Dishes

Liver, when thinly sliced is ideal for quick cooking. Some may not favour kidneys and liver at the guéridon because of cooking smells but as far as calves' and sheep's liver are concerned perhaps an important consideration is that they are better suited for simple modes of service. Good results may, however, be achieved by deglazing the chafing dish after quickly sauté-ing the liver with jus lié and a fortified wine such as sherry or Madeira. Alternatively, a piquant finishing using a wine vinegar reduction and a garnish of gherkin cut in julienne.

Chicken livers cut into small collops also lend themselves to sauté-ing with subsequent deglazing of the pan with jus lié or demi-glace and flavouring of brandy or fortified wines.

VEGETABLES

Vegetables are all too often a neglected feature in restaurants in the British Isles. The point has been made, however, when discussing the use of the table lamp in earlier chapters that this is not an apparatus for repairing the deficiencies of the kitchen. Thus the lamp should not be used to reheat cooling vegetables. There may, however, be a case in some types of restaurant operation for vegetables intentionally to be prepared slightly undercooked in the kitchen so that they may be completed au beurre at the table.

Some of the rarer and more expensive vegetables, particularly asparagus and artichokes, are, of course, featured as individual items. Traditionally they followed a main course but nowadays are commonly used as an introductory one. Asparagus and artichokes may be served warm with warm sauces (particularly melted butters and hollandaise and its derivatives) but also with cold sauces of vinaigrette style. These latter obviously afford an opportunity for a maître d'hôtel to prepare the sauce at the side table. Dressings of this kind are, of course, further outlined in the salad section.

The "do-it-yourself" trend already reflected in the restaurant by fondue services may be given further application in providing accompaniments for asparagus and artichoke à la flamande. For this service each diner is provided from the guéridon with half a hard boiled egg, with a small sauceboat of melted butter and a small tray or plate of condiments. Guests tend to enjoy finishing their own sauce by mashing the egg with a fork, mixing with the beurre fondue and adding their own seasoning. Equally, of course, waiters may prepare their own accompaniments in this style. Further elaborations using grated Parmesan and chopped herbs for top garnishing will, no doubt, suggest themselves.

SWEETS

The range of sweets which can be completed or prepared from the guéridon is almost unlimited. For example, much may be done with fine fruits in season both fresh and poached. In Britain pears and apples peeled and cored and lightly pre-prepared in syrup are, if just cooked à point, excellent for filling with fresh cream interestingly garnished—with, for example, chopped chocolate, praliné, slices of ginger and other preserved fruits and so on. Alternatively pastry creams with similar blends and garnishes may be used. Marron (chestnut) purée is also suitable for filling cavities of fruit left by the core or stone.

There are endless possibilities in the composing of fruit salads and in dressing dishes with an ice cream base.

For the best sweet culmination of a meal, however, it is likely that simply dressed fruits using choice liqueurs will be preferred. The following two examples are intended to suggest the approach rather than the range.

FRAISES ROYALE

Ingredients for 4 covers:

1½ lb. hulled strawberries	2 measures Van der Hum
Caster sugar	2 measures Kirsch
Crème chantilly	Juice of 1 orange

Method:

1. Place the strawberries in a glass bowl on the guéridon.
2. Sprinkle fairly lavishly with sugar.
3. Add a measure of liqueur and orange juice and toss.
4. Repeat this until all liqueurs have been used.
5. Serve on dessert plates and offer the cream.

Familiar, but nevertheless invariably popular, strawberry dishes from the guéridon include also:

FRAISES ROMANOFF

Hulled strawberries macerated with fine sugar, curaçao and lemon juice and either topped or blended with whipped or Chantilly cream.

ETON MESS

Hulled strawberries macerated in caster sugar, lightly fork-broken and blended with whipped cream.

MINGAUX RENNAIS

This whipped strawberry cream of Brittany may also suggest adaptations.

FRAMBOISES BOULEVARDIER

Mise en place:

Raspberries	Sauce Melba
Whipped cream	Dubonnet

Caster sugar   Kirsch
Icing sugar

Set two silver timbales on ice. In one place the raspberries
thoroughly turned in caster sugar. In the other timbale blend together the whipped cream, sauce Melba and a glass of Dubonnet
and a dash of kirsch to form a flowing sauce, well coloured by the
Melba.

Mask this coloured and flavoured cream over the raspberries,
dust with icing sugar and serve.

PÊCHES À LA ROYALE

Mise en place:

Peaches (poached in syrup)   Brandy
Strawberries   Whipped cream

Originally this dish, as a French speciality of the Touraine area,
was made with fraises du bois (wild strawberries) but where these
are not available ordinary cultivated strawberries give satisfactory
results.

Method:

    1. Sprinkle the strawberries lightly with caster sugar and
allow them to macerate (desirably, leave these to stand during
the service of the preliminary part of the meal).

    2. Crush the strawberries in the sugar with a fork, adding
brandy.

    3. Fold in whipped cream.

    4. Mask the peaches with the strawberry and cream
mixture.

Sabayon (or Zabaglione) is rather troublesome and tedious to
make at side table but syllabubs (or wine and liqueur flavoured
creams) may suggest possibilities for service alone or in conjunction with compôtes or fruit salads.

Apart from the examples of dishes in the foregoing notes other
thoughts may be afforded from the dishes listed and the ideas
proposed for flambé dishes in the next chapter. In the case of both
sweet and savoury items, for example, some of the flambé dishes
can be adapted for preparation without actual flaring and many
kinds of hot sweets using the pancake as the basis can be guéridon
served without actual flaming.

CHAPTER 5

SAVOURY DISHES FLAMED

Earlier chapters have already stressed that the visual attractions of flambé dishes constitute a major part of their gastronomic appeal. Because such dishes play an important part in promoting business, feeding the ego of the guest as well as his appetite, and adding small, dramatic touches to the atmosphere of the restaurant, it need not follow that the purely culinary side should be treated with cynicism. Whilst it is true that most dishes, both simple and complex, will tend to be better prepared under the skilled hands of the chef in a properly equipped kitchen there are, nevertheless, restaurateurs, maîtres d'hôtel and even amateurs amongst restaurant and hotel owners who can cultivate the skills necessary both to cook dishes "in the room" which require only a short time or to complete the cooking of partially prepared items sent from the kitchen.

Flambé dishes can enjoy one or two great advantages to offset any disadvantages; for such food is clearly freshly cooked, its ingredients plainly seen to be of good quality and it may be served piping hot. These are not trivial factors and explain why many gourmets as well as those guests who simply seek fuss and entertainment appreciate many flambé dishes.

General Points

Before considering the recipes which follow, some points about flambé work which have a general application may be made. There are two broad divisions for such dishes. First, there are those mainly cooked behind the scenes and brought into the room only for the final flaring process. These are usually items like game birds and poultry which quite clearly take far too long and use cookery equipment quite different from that practicable for the room. Dishes of this kind are generally simple to complete and serve.

Secondly, there are those foods which, other than for pre-preparation in the larder or kitchen in order that there should be no delay in the actual cooking process, are virtually prepared from start to finish in the restaurant. It follows that almost any dish which only requires pan cooking for a short period may be prepared in this way; but it is equally clear that not all foods are suitable for such treatment and certainly not all are suitable for flambé-ing. For example, some of the dishes of the south of France and of the Basque area are pan cooked using fairly rapid processes, but the extent to which the more pungent aromas like garlic may be permitted to penetrate a restaurant has to be considered. Thus choice narrows not merely to foods capable of being cooked quickly but foods whose cooking odours are neither too strong nor too penetrating.

Amongst foods generally thought suitable for finishing or cooking rapidly in the restaurant and in this style, sweet items predominate. They are ideal because their cooking perfumes are generally agreeable. They are separately considered in the following chapter. As far as savoury work is concerned, meats such as minute steaks, veal and pork escalopes, chicken suprêmes, kidneys and liver (particularly chicken livers) are suitable for quick pan work, but here again there is the problem that the smell of cooking kidneys is not always acceptable to diners at adjoining tables. Fish, too, is capable of being cooked rapidly, but many fish items must be excluded on the score of cooking smell. The most usual exceptions are finishing previously cooked shell fish such as lobster and scampi. These can generally be flambé-d without occasioning nuisance to other diners. On their south coast the French do "finish" fish by flaming to yield specialities like *Loups de Mediterranée grillés et flambés au fenouil*. What the French do to the "wolf fish" may suggest treatments for our own hauls.

The significant point behind the foregoing observations is that the recipe section following is not merely meant to afford working formulae. It is rather hoped that the recipes may stimulate inventiveness in adapting specialities and will encourage further individual touches in creating "specialities of the house".

Indeed, one of the positive points in favour of flambé cooking is the scope it gives to the individual "performer". In adapting or exploiting the recipe ideas, however, careful thought must be given to the question of suitability of chosen items from the point of view of cooking time, manageability in the pan, freedom from penetrating (not merely unpleasant) cooking odours.

SOUPS

Soups hardly lend themselves to flambé treatment though it is possible to ladle flaming liquor over tureen or tasse in their service, especially in the case of clear soups. Such treatments may, perhaps, be regarded as more gimmick than gastronomic but an example is:

CONSOMMÉ FLAMBÉ AU XÉRÈS

Mise en place at the guéridon:

Tureen of consommé on hotplate, lamp, consommé tasses and undercovers, ladle, sherry.

To serve and flame:

1. Portion consommé into the cups.
2. Heat the bowl of the soup ladle over the flame and add a measure of sherry.
3. Again place the ladle over the flame, and as it heats tilt the ladle to flame the vaporising sherry.
4. Ladle the flaming sherry carefully over the surface of the cupped consommé. Serve immediately and whilst still alight.

SHELL FISH

SAUCE HOMARD—LOBSTER SAUCE

Lobster sauce, prepared in the kitchen, is required for dishes such as *Crevettes roses flambées au cognac*, *Homard flambé au pastis* (which both follow in this section) and for other similar dishes.

For 1 pint:

$\frac{1}{2}$ lb. lobster shell (including cooked coral and spawn)	1 oz. bacon scraps
	4 or 5 peppercorns
$\frac{1}{4}$ clove crushed garlic	$1\frac{1}{4}$ pints fish stock
$\frac{1}{4}$ lb. tomato concassé	$\frac{1}{2}$ glass white wine

1 bouquet garni

2 tablesp. tomato purée

1 tablesp. diced carrot

1 tablesp. chopped onion

1 tablesp. brandy

1 oz. flour

1 oz. butter

Salt

Method:

1. Thoroughly crush the lobster shells, coral and spawn (using the mortar).

2. Sauté them quickly in butter together with the carrot, onion and bacon scraps.

3. Stir in the flour and continue to cook for a few moments without allowing the flour to colour.

4. Blend in the tomato concassé and purée, stock and white wine stirring all the time to achieve a smooth consistency.

5. Bring to the boil, skim and add peppercorns with the bouquet garni.

6. Simmer gently for 1 hour, allowing one-third reduction.

7. Skim as required, strain, adjust the seasoning and complete with the brandy.

CREVETTES ROSES FLAMBÉES AU COGNAC

Peeled, cooked prawns

Butter

Cognac

Lobster sauce (recipe above)

Cream

Salt, pepper

Method:

1. Melt the butter over a low flame and when hot add the prawns.

2. Allow the prawns to heat in the butter then tilt the pan slightly away from the body and add the cognac to the surface and flambé.

3. Add lobster sauce, increase the flame and simmer.

4. Add the cream and allow to heat thoroughly without actually boiling. Complete the seasoning.

5. Serve from the pan but precede with pilaff rice.

Scampi, shrimps, sliced lobster meat and crayfish may be similarly prepared.

Accompaniment: Pilaff rice.

SCAMPI FLAMBÉS À LA CRÈME

2 oz. butter	½ glass Chablis
Salt, pepper	1 measure cognac
3 tomatoes concassé	2 tablesp. cream
½ pint scampi (peeled)	Paprika
2 finely chopped shallots	

Method:

1. Melt the butter, sweat the finely chopped shallots; when softening but not coloured, add the scampi, tossing and turning them over moderate flame, sprinkling with a little pepper.

2. When thoroughly hot, add the cognac and flame.

3. Add half a wine glass of white wine and the tomato concassé, raise the flame and allow to reduce.

4. Finish with cream, adjust seasoning, sprinkle with paprika and serve.

Accompaniments: Pilaff rice or dish in warm vol au vent cases.

SCAMPI BOULEVARD

For one cover:

4 oz. lightly floured scampi	1 fl. oz. brandy
2 fl. oz. dry vermouth	⅛ pint fresh cream

Mr George Mulvey at Glasgow's Boulevard Hotel prepares this as follows:

1. Melt a little butter in the blazer and when hot add scampi and dry vermouth.

2. Increase heat to seal the scampi and reduce the liquor.

3. Flame in the brandy and extinguish flames with the fresh cream.

4. Reduce resulting sauce and serve on bed of rice garnished with chopped yellow peppers.

Accompaniments: Previously cooked rice, garnished with chopped yellow peppers.

Lobster

The flesh from cooked lobster (or langouste) cut into neat collops is well suited for simple modes of flambé. Basically all that is required is to melt butter in the blazer, heat the lobster thoroughly, add the spirit (or liqueur) of choice and flame. The finishing sauce may be made by deglazing with cream (or a suitable basic fish sauce) with or without further flavourings such as curry powders, paprika, other herbs and spices.

Whisky goes well as a flambé agent with lobster. The following examples show possibilities.

HOMARD FLAMBÉ À MA FAÇON

1 lobster	1 dessertsp. oil
2 oz. butter	½ shallot (minced)
1 liqueur glass armagnac	2 tablesp. cream
3 tomatoes concassés	½ clove garlic

In the kitchen:

1. Separate the meat from a boiled lobster and cut into collops.

2. Peel, de-pip and chop the tomatoes, finely chop the shallot and the crushed garlic.

In the room:

1. Heat the oil over a steady flame and sauté the shallot and garlic.

2. Before the shallot colours add the butter and when hot tip in the lobster.

3. Tilting the pan add the armagnac and flame.

4. Baste the pieces thoroughly with the flamed liquor at the same time adding the tomato concassé.

5. Adjust the seasoning and complete by adding the cream, serving when hot but before the cream and liquor actually boil.

HOMARD FLAMBÉ AU PASTIS

Cooked lobster (in slices)	Cream
Finely diced onion (brunoise)	Pastis (Pernod, white or yellow
Finely sliced mushroom	or Ricard)
Butter	Lobster sauce (recipe page 58)

Method:

1. Sweat the diced onion in butter over low flame without colouring adding the mushrooms just as the onions become soft.

2. Add the lobster sauce and, when simmering, add the cooked lobster meat.

3. Tilt the pan, add the pastis and flambé.
4. Finish with cream, allowing the dish to reheat without boiling.

Accompaniments: Pilaff rice or bouchées or vol au vent cases, or puff paste fleurons.

POULTRY

POUSSIN FLAMBÉ À LA FINE CHAMPAGNE

Poussin	Fine champagne
Mushrooms	Jus lié
Salt, pepper	Finely chopped onions
Butter	Cream

In the kitchen:

1. Roast or poële the poussin in the usual way and send to the table. Cut into half either in the kitchen or at the table.

In the room:

1. Keeping the chicken warm and under cover, melt the butter in the chafing dish, add the chopped onion and sweat.
2. When the onion is soft, add a little jus lié and seasoning and when simmering lay in the poussin.
3. Add the brandy and flame.
4. Circle with cream blending to form a sauce and ensure that the poussin is thoroughly masked with the sauce.

Suggested accompaniments: Wild rice, pommes parisienne and haricot vert au beurre.

Note: Almost any cocotte or casserole poultry dish may be flamed when presented at table. There is, for example, even a version of that old friend *Coq au vin flambé à la fine bourgogne.*

SUPRÊME DE VOLAILLE GRAND MARC

Chicken suprêmes, as observed in the previous chapter, are suited for relatively quick cookery on the lamp and are capable of individual treatments. Featured by Mr George Mulvey at Glasgow's Boulevard Hotel, for example, is *Suprême de volaille grand marc.* For this dish the suprême is sauté-d in butter with chopped onion, tomatoes and mushrooms; then flamed with brandy and extinguished with cream.

CANETON FLAMBÉ AU CALVADOS

Freshly roasted duckling   Jus lié
Apples   Calvados
Butter   Salt
Cream   Pepper

In the kitchen:

1. Roast the duckling.
2. Prepare peeled apples in thick slices or quarters and quickly and lightly sauté in butter, arranging them to cover the bottom of a chafing dish or cocotte.
3. Carve the duckling and arrange on the bed of sauté-d apples.
4. Deglaze the roasting tray with jus lié and strain into sauceboat.

In the room:

1. Ensure that the dish is thoroughly hot by placing on the lamp.
2. Pour over the hot deglacé-ing liquor from the sauceboat.
3. Add the calvados and flare.

Accompaniments: Pommes château, petits pois à la française.

CANETON FLAMBÉ À L'ORANGE—DUCKLING FLAVOURED WITH ORANGE

1 × 2 lb. roasted duckling   Jus lié (lightly thickened roast
Orange   duck gravy)
Lemon $\frac{1}{2}$ glass white wine
Curaçao

In the kitchen:

1. In a quick oven (425°–450° F.) roast the duckling on a bed of mirepoix, basting and turning at intervals.
2. During the 1 hour (approximately) of this process, finely pare away the zest of the orange and cut into fine julienne (a little lemon zest julienne may also be added).
3. Blanch and refresh and strain the julienne.
4. Complete the peeling of the oranges by removing skin and pith completely and then cut out the fruit in pith-free slivers or segments.

5. Squeeze the core and pith for juice.

6. When the duckling is roasted, remove and keep warm.

7. Strain away excess fat from the roasting pan and then deglaze over heat with jus lié.

8. Carve the duck and arrange in chafing dish or fireproof vessel, scatter with the julienne and moisten with a little of the sauce.

In the room:

1. Place the dish of duckling on low flame.

2. Have remaining sauce and accompanying salads and vegetables "en place" on sideboard or guéridon hotplate.

3. Flambé the duck with curaçao and serve immediately with accompaniments.

Variations: Specific forms of curaçao, such as Grand Marnier or Cointreau, may of course be used. A blend of curaçao and cognac in equal quantities is also recommended.

Accompaniments: Pommes soufflées, tossed salad.

CANETON FLAMBÉ AUX ANANAS, CANETON FLAMBÉ AUX
  CERISES

At Gafners in Paris a duck dish in similar tradition to the *à l'orange* treatment above, effectively substitutes pineapple. Cherries also (often associated with duck in the Montmorency garnish) are appropriate and permit variation of liqueur.

GAME

BECASSE FLAMBÉE—FLAMED WOODCOCK

Ingredients per woodcock:

1 woodcock	1 oz. foie gras
1 strip pork back fat	1 croûton
1 oz. butter	Salt, pepper
½ glass Madeira	1 measure cognac

In the kitchen:

1. Prepare the woodcock in the usual way, i.e. without drawing the intestines, season, truss and "bard" with back fat.

2. Roast briskly (450° F.) for 10 to 15 minutes so that the bird is nicely coloured but remains underdone.

3. Deglaze the roast pan with good, brown stock or consommé to form a roast gravy.

4. Withdraw the intestines, chop them and sauté in butter.

5. Mix with the roast gravy and pass through the sieve.

6. Send to the room.

In the room:

1. Keeping the bird warm, melt in the blazer a little butter and add the purée or parfait of foie gras.

2. Stir in the roast gravy and Madeira to form a sauce.

3. Tilt the blazer, add cognac and ignite.

4. Retain the bird whole (but halve or cut it if desired by guest), coat with the sauce.

Accompaniments: Pommes chips, salade de saison, fonds d'artichauts filled with foie gras and topped with sliver of truffle.

At one time a woodcock feast was held in Mons and Liège (in similar tradition to the annual Colchester feast of oysters in Britain). Whether this continues or not one of the old customs seems to foreshadow the flambé fashion; for each guest had his own little wax candle to frizzle the woodcock's head before it was eaten.

Bécassine (snipe) may be similarly prepared and served as woodcock.

RABLE DE LIÈVRE DU POMPIER—FIREMAN'S SADDLE OF HARE

Saddle of hare   Demi glace
Red currant jelly   Butter
Salt, pepper   Armagnac

In the kitchen:

1. Marinate the saddle in a good red wine marinade for at least 3 days and strain.

2. Fry the saddle steadily in butter and oil until well coloured but slightly underdone.

3. Deglaze the pan with demi-glace and strained marinade (in equal quantities) to form sauce. Season. Send to the room.

In the room:

1. Melt butter in the chafing dish, add red currant jelly and then the sauce. Adjust seasoning.

2. Lay in the saddles of hare, turning to coat well with sauce.

3. Add the armagnac and flare.

Accompaniments: Red currant jelly or Bar-le-duc jam; broccoli spears au beurre; pommes dauphine.

VENISON TENDERLOIN TAM O' SHANTER (FILLET OF VENISON FLAMED IN WHISKY)

2 oz. butter
1 measure Scotch whisky
½ gill slightly thickened game gravy

Filet mignon from saddles of venison
1 oz. good liver paste
½ glass sherry

In the kitchen:

1. Remove the fillet or tenderloin from the saddle of venison and trim it free of fat and membrane.

2. If large, the mignon may be cut into two or more slices with a horizontal, diagonal cut. In any case, flatten the mignon slightly with the cutlet bat.

In the room:

1. Sprinkle the venison with salt and pepper whilst heating butter in blazer.

2. Lay in the venison and sauté over steady heat until browned on both sides. (Usually the meat is preferred underdone.)

3. Tilt the pan, add measure of whisky and flame. Whilst flaming draw the mignons to the back or handle side of the pan and with the pan still slightly tilted forward extinguish the flame by adding jus lié.

4. Add in the liver paste stirring to form a smooth consistency.

5. Add the sherry and allow the sauce to simmer with the mignons brought forward to become thoroughly masked with the mixture.

Accompaniments: Red currant jelly, roast potatoes, grilled mushrooms, tossed green salad.

MEAT

Flambé-d Roasts

Other than small game birds such as those treated earlier in this chapter, roasts are not dominantly associated with the flambé process. Clearly, however, small roasting pieces (including other poultry, ortolans, quail and game birds) which are normally carved and served from the guéridon can be flamed prior to such treatment from the side table. Small sections of contrefilet, the fillet of beef itself and carré of lamb are, when roasted, suitable for basting with flaming spirit or a jus lié topped with flaming liqueur. This may be done not only over the whole, uncarved joint but alternatively after the carving has been completed.

A choice piece of fillet lends itself to flaming as, for example, *Filet de bœuf piqué et flambé à la fine champagne.*

A preparation of best end of lamb, the crown roast, may be thought especially suitable for this type of treatment because of its stylish appearance. A roast crown of lamb with the interior complete with its vegetable garnish can most suitably receive flaming liquor before it is cut. At Chicago's Drake Hotel, for example, such a dish, *Couronne d'agneau flambé*, has been featured with a flambé sauce devised by Chef Kauffman.

Clearly for larger joints there is less opportunity for service in this style but when a carving voiture is featured in the restaurant, it is possible to ladle a spoonful of flaming brandy over a portion of roast meat. For example, a service of *Tranche de gigot flambée* (slice of leg of lamb flamed) is by no means unknown.

Monkey Gland Steak

This flambé-d minute fillet was developed in the 1920's and early 1930's when the so-called "monkey gland" experiments in surgery for rejuvenation was still a talking point. The dish was particularly associated with the Adelphi Hotel, Liverpool and the Central Hotel, Glasgow and especially with the name of Luigi, for many years maître d'hôtel in the Central's Malmaison restaurant.

Other versions have been offered including chefs' elaborations and one which captures the "rejuvenation theme" by sewing up oysters in the meat in "Carpet Bag Steak" style. But the following "in the room" presentation is generally accepted today.

Ingredients:

Fillet steak	Dijon mustard
Butter	Chopped parsley
Salt, pepper	Worcestershire sauce
Chopped shallot	Cognac

Method:

1. Fillet steak should be cut thinly and further flattened by the bat prior to entry in the room.

2. Whilst butter is melting in the chafing dish season the steak with salt and pepper from the mill and smear with Dijon mustard.

3. Add the onion to the heated butter and cook. As the onions soften turn up the flame, add the steak.

4. When the steak has been cooked on each side add a dash of Worcestershire sauce, then add the brandy and flame.

5. Extinguish the flame by covering with the lid, sprinkle with parsley and serve.

Accompaniments: Baked jacket potato, broccoli spears or pommes pont neuf and tossed green salad.

Minute and Butterfly Steaks

Cuts from the fillet and contrefilet batted thin for quick cookery are ideal for flambé purposes. *Entrecôtes minute* (from the contre-filet) are well known as are fillet cuts flattened for Monkey Gland (above) and Steak Diane (below). Also of interest are Butterfly steaks which are, in effect, one inch thick tournedos cut through to leave only a small amount of connecting meat and then opened, flattened and batted to form two wings.

Minute steaks may even be formed from finely minced beef-steak to form "Hamburgerettes".

STEAK DIANE

Fillet steak	Finely diced mushroom
Worcestershire sauce	Butter Parsley
Finely chopped onion	Cognac

Method:

1. Ensure that the thinly cut fillet steaks are well flattened with cutlet bat.

2. In the room, season them with salt and pepper from the mill whilst the butter is melting over the réchaud.

3. Sauté the thin fillets briskly and keep hot on a covered plate.

4. Sauté the chopped onion in butter and as it begins to take colour add the mushrooms.

5. Return the steaks turning them in the mushrooms and onions and adjust the seasoning.

6. Add a dash of Worcestershire sauce and flame with brandy.

Accompaniments: Pommes sautées, tomatoes farcies, French salad.

Note: Steak Diane does not appear in the old French culinary classics and it is, indeed, a dish which has emerged in recent years as a result of the cult of the lamp. No wonder that methods and recorded recipes widely differ. One substantial cookery book does, indeed, cite a version in which the steak is grilled and sent to table with a sauce made from "boiled red wine and peppers" which, when reduced, has cream added. Many lamp "magicians" do little other than deglaze the pan after sauté-ing the steak with cream (usually sour cream) flavour with Worcestershire sauce and flare. Minced shallots, red wine reduction or a dash of sherry or cognac are used according to the preference of the "lamp operator".

Because Diane (Diana) was goddess of the chase or hunt, it has also been suggested that the dish may originally have featured venison steak.

Veal Escalopes

Escalopes (and piccata) cut from the cushion (also from the fillet and saddle) trimmed of gristle, batted flat and nicely shaped are ideal for lamp cookery. Such cuts of veal should, in any case, be cooked rapidly to avoid toughening and drying of the meat.

PICCATA ANNA MARGARETTA

For this dish featured at Glasgow's Boulevard Hotel, Mr George Mulvey's recipe is:

Ingredients per person:

    4 oz. fillet steak beaten very flat
    1 clove garlic

1 onion cut Lyonnaise style
2 fl. oz. sweet Chianti
1 fl. oz. Fior d'Alpe
1 oz. Mozarella cheese
Sliced, previously cooked pimento

Method:

1. Melt one half ounce of butter in pan with a little olive oil.

2. Add Lyonnaise onions and cook until golden brown.

3. Rub steak with garlic and season to taste.

4. Increase heat of pan and place in steak.

5. Reduce heat when steak is sealed; then add sweet Chianti and reduce.

6. Complete cooking process by sprinkling the steak with the cheese and fold. Flame with Fior d'Alpe.

7. Garnish with heated pimento and serve on a bed of previously cooked egg noodles.

ESCALOPE DE VEAU SMITANE

2 × 4 oz. veal escalopes	Finely diced onion
Butter	Cognac
Seasoning	Cream (fresh or sour as liked)

Method:

1. Melt the butter, add the onion and sweat over moderate flame.

2. When the onion softens, increase the flame and add the seasoned collops of veal.

3. Cook the veal both sides (about 2 minutes each side is enough for well batted collops).

4. Remove the meat to a warm, silver "flat".

5. Deglaze the pan with cream (some like to add a little sherry at this stage) and season.

6. Whilst this sauce heats gently, add cognac to the escalopes and flame.

7. Extinguish the flame by pouring over the hot cream sauce and serve.

Accompaniments: Nouilles au beurre or rice or pommes persil-lées with tossed green pepper and lettuce salad, haricot verts or epinards en branches or broccoli spears.

ESCALOPE DE VEAU ELIZABETH MARIE

For this speciality of Glasgow's Boulevard Hotel, Mr George Mulvey's recipe is:

Ingredients per person:

3½-4 oz. escalope (from veal fillet)
One small clove of garlic
1½ oz. finely chopped onion
6 asparagus tips
2 fl. oz. sweet sherry
1 fl. oz. Bacardi
⅛ pint fresh cream

Method:

1. Rub pan with garlic.
2. Add butter, melt and add chopped onion, seasoning to taste.
3. Cook onions gently until golden brown.
4. Increase heat of pan and place flattened veal escalopes in the pan.
5. Seal escalope and then reduce heat.
6. Pour sweet sherry over the escalopes and cook until liquor has been reduced.
7. When cooking process has been almost completed flambé the escalope in Bacardi (or other white rum) and extinguish flames with fresh cream.
8. Complete the cooking process by reducing the resulting sauce to a reasonably viscous consistency.
9. Garnish with heated asparagus tips and serve.

GAMMON RASHER SINGAPORE

This dish, devised and featured by Mr H. R. Freeman, Lecturer in restaurant service, is prepared as follows:

Ingredients for 2 covers:

1 × ½-inch-thick gammon rasher (approx. 12 oz.)
½ sauceboat demi-glace
Large slice or 2 small slices pineapple (preferably fresh)

Pepper
¼ lb. sliced mushrooms
Butter
Tobasco sauce
Rum

Method:

1. Keep hot the gammon rasher, previously grilled in the kitchen.

2. Melt the butter over the réchaud and add the mushrooms finely sliced.

3. When nearly cooked add demi-glace, season with salt, pepper, a dash of Tobasco, squeeze of lemon and add pine-apple.

4. Add the rum, flame at the moment that the guests are served with the gammon, and top the rashers with the pine-apple and with the mushroom sauce.

Suggested accompaniments: Pommes persillées, haricots verts au beurre.

HIGHLAND HAM STEAK

2 gammon steaks grilled (or sauté-d)
1 tablesp. single malt whisky
1 glass hock
1 gill cream

Butter
Seasoning
Scottish tomatoes (pipped, peeled and sliced)

Method:

1. Melt the butter over low flame and lay in the ham which has previously been grilled or pan broiled. Ensure that the ham is hot.

2. Add the whisky and flame.

3. Remove the ham and put to one side on a réchaud while the sauce is being made as follows.

4. Rinse the pan with the hock, turning up the flame so that the wine reduces rapidly.

5. Add a further knob of butter; then the tomato.

6. When all is thoroughly hot, add the cream, combining thoroughly over low flame to ensure the sauce becomes hot without boiling.

7. Mask the ham steaks with sauce.

Accompaniments: Belted potatoes (pommes en robe de chambre), purée of spinach.

BATONS DE JAMBON FLAMBÉS DES BONS-FRÈRES

Boiled gammon cut in batons (or "fingers")	Wine glass demi-glace
	1 teasp. vinegar
Butter	Chopped gherkin
1 dessertsp. red currant jelly	Salt, pepper, paprika
1 glass cognac and Benedictine (mixed in equal parts)	1 dessertsp. sugar
	1 glass burgundy

Method:

1. Melt the butter over a moderate flame, add the sugar and teaspoon of vinegar and allow to caramelise.

2. Add gradually the burgundy and red currant jelly.

3. Add the demi-glace and, when simmering, add the chopped gherkin.

4. Tip in the batons of ham and allow to combine thoroughly with the sauce.

5. Tilt the pan, gently add the cognac and Benedictine previously mixed and warmed and flame.

6. Extinguish the flame with cream, blend thoroughly, adjust the seasoning, dust with paprika and serve.

Accompaniments: Nouilles au beurre, haricots panachés.

ESCALOPES DE PORC MAUPASSANT

Pork fillets	Butter
Calvados	Syrup
Apples	Lemon

In the kitchen:

1. Trim the pork fillets free of fat and membrane. Cut into half horizontally and lightly flatten with the bat.

2. Peel and core the apples and poach quickly and lightly in syrup, to which has been added lemon juice. (Do not permit the halved apples to cook through.)

In the room:

1. Melt the butter over steady flame and sauté the seasoned pork fillets until they are browned on each side.

2. Remove to a warm dish and adding further butter as required to the pan, heat and colour the well drained apple halves.

3. Remove and then place with the pork fillets.

4. To the hot pan residue add a measure of Calvados and flame.

5. Extinguish the flames with the cream and continuing to heat gently combine the cream with the pan residue.

6. Adjust seasoning, pour the cream sauce over the pork and apples, dust with paprika and serve.

Garnish with: Fond d'artichaut clamart (artichoke bottoms piped with purée of fresh peas) and pommes château.

ROGNONS DE VEAU FLAMBÉS À L'ARMAGNAC

2 veal kidneys	2 tablesp. (approx.) jus lié
1 glass white wine	1 tablesp. tomato concassé
½ teasp. meat glaze	1 teasp. chopped parsley
1 oz. butter	1 measure armagnac
2 tablesp. fresh cream	

In the kitchen:

1. Prepare the veal kidneys in the usual way, slicing in half and retaining a little of the surrounding suet.

2. Sauter au beurre, cooking until browned but still slightly underdone. Deglaze the pan with white wine and jus lié.

3. Send the kidneys to the room in a warm dish with a sauceboat of the deglazing liquor and raviers or small dishes of remaining ingredients.

In the room:

1. At the guéridon slice the kidneys whilst a little butter is melting in the blazer or chafing dish from which the kidneys have been removed.

2. Return the kidneys to the chafing dish. Add the concassé tomatoes, the deglazing liquor, meat glaze, seasoning and simmer.

3. Tilt the pan, add the warmed armagnac and flame.

4. Extinguish the flames with cream, thoroughly combine, sprinkle with parsley and serve.

Accompaniments: Spoon the kidneys over segments of sauté-d aubergines or over rice or nouilles.

Rognon de veau en pyjama

More than one French restaurant has accorded this fanciful title to a lamp treatment of veal kidney. "Pyjama" is merely descriptive of the neat border of suet left surrounding the lengthwise, halved kidney. The method is similar to that described for Rognons de veau flambés above and involves sauté-ing for about three minutes on the non-fat side and a little longer on the fatty side. Subsequently flambé-ing may be effected with cognac, armagnac or other marc, or with whisky or liqueurs to choice.

VEAL KIDNEYS FLAMED IN WARDROOM FASHION

2 veal kidneys	1 dessertsp. oil
Liqueur glass Plymouth gin	1 oz. mushroom (thickly sliced)
½ gill cream	Clove
2 oz. butter	Salt, pepper
Bayleaf	

Method:

1. Cut kidneys in half lengthwise and trim off all but a neat surrounding of fat. Season with salt and pepper.

2. Heat the oil, add the butter and when hot, sauté the kidneys, fat side first over moderate flame.

3. As the kidneys should be rather underdone, they may be turned as soon as they are adequately coloured.

4. On turning, and once the non-fat side has been sealed, add the mushrooms and complete the cooking.

5. Pour off the fat leaving only the savoury pan residue.

6. Add the gin, flame and extinguish with the pan cover.

7. Add the cream and blend thoroughly with the pan residue. When hot adjust the seasoning and serve.

Accompaniments: Baked, jacket potatoes, grilled tomatoes, French beans.

LAMBS KIDNEYS FLARED WITH ARMAGNAC

1 dessertsp. oil	1 or 2 oz. sliced mushrooms
1 dessertsp. finely chopped	1 glass armagnac

shallot	1 gill cream
4–6 lambs kidneys	Salt, pepper
1 oz. butter	

In the kitchen:

    1. Trim the kidneys free of gristle, membrane and fat.
    2. Halve them and slice thinly.

In the room:

    1. Melt the oil and butter; add the seasoned kidneys and a dessertspoonful of finely chopped shallots.
    2. Add the mushrooms thinly sliced.
    3. Add the armagnac and flame: then extinguish with the lid cover.
    4. Add the cream, blend well with the pan contents and when thoroughly hot adjust seasoning and serve.

Variants: Top the finished dish with julienne of truffle.
Accompaniments: Rice pilaff, nouilles au beurre, riced potatoes with appropriate green vegetables or tossed salad.

For *Brochette of Kidneys* see Chapter 8.

RIS DE VEAU FLAMBÉ

4 sweetbreads	1 gill cream
4 heart-shaped croûtons	1 measure cognac
Salt, pepper	½ glass sherry
2 oz. mushrooms	Chopped parsley
2 oz. butter	

In the kitchen:

    1. Simmer the sweetbreads in good stock for 15–20 minutes then drain and allow to cool between 2 plates under pressure from weights.
    2. When cold, trim away membrane and cut each sweetbread into four finger lengths.

In the room:

    1. Melt the butter over a moderate flame, add the seasoned sweetbreads and toss or turn until they are beginning to colour.

2. Add the brandy and flare.

3. Extinguish the flame with the cover, add the mushrooms and half glass of sherry and allow to simmer.

4. Add cream and adjust seasoning.

5. When thoroughly hot, add heart-shaped croûtons of butter, fried bread and bouquets of chopped parsley and serve.

Accompaniments: Pommes rissolées, pointes d'asperges au beurre or other green vegetable or salad in season.

MUSHROOMS

Other types of fungi may be treated similarly to cèpes as in the example below. Variations may be effected by adding tomato concassé, pimento or green pepper strips and by further herb, spice or sauce flavouring. Other liqueurs or spirits may naturally be essayed for flaming.

CÈPES FLAMBÉS À LA BORDELAISE

1 can cèpes	1 oz. butter
Chopped parsley	1 tablesp. cognac
1 tablesp. oil	1 clove garlic
1 tablesp. finely chopped shallot	

In the kitchen:

Rinse the cèpes in cold water, strain and slice thickly, finely chopping stems.

In the room:

1. Melt oil and sweat the shallot.

2. Add butter and when melted add the cèpes.

3. When thoroughly hot, add cognac and flame. Extinguish the flame.

4. Add finely chopped, crushed garlic and the cèpes stems finely chopped. Complete seasoning and add the parsley.

5. Ensure that all is thoroughly blended and hot.

6. Serve with grilled rump, point or sirloin steaks or, with a little cream blended in, the cèpes may be served as a savoury on croûtons or hot canapés.

CHAPTER 6

CRÊPES, FRUITS AND OTHER FLAMBÉ SWEETS

The preceding chapter stressed the suitability of sweet items for cooking in the room and for flambé treatment. Suitability rests on two important factors: speed and pleasant or neutral cooking smells. Moreover, sugar sprinkled during flaring also encourages blue, dancing flames which are generally considered pleasing. For sweet items, factors of care and simplicity, therefore, go far to explain the heavy concentration of attention as far as lamp work is concerned, on pancakes and on fruit. Because of the widespread use of these items it is thought appropriate in this separate section to consider them together with a few other ideas for sweets and puddings capable of being flamed at the table.

CRÊPES

There are curious snobberies and inverted snobberies about food and drink. Enjoyment or otherwise, for example, of champagne seems often to be curiously affected by considerations other than genuine gastronomic ones.

In the modern restaurant era the basically simple pancake has been promoted as a major sweet dessert and crêpe Suzette, the most famous of all the dramatised, flambé-d, versions of pancake, has become as well known, even to non-gastronomes, as has pêche Melba. It is all too easy to decry the popular and to assume disdainful attitudes about universally demanded foods but the fact remains that the pancake has proved itself a most suitable main element for flambé sweet dishes and, indeed, generally for elaborations as puddings which have commanded universal appeal.

There are clearly many reasons for the success of the pancake in lamp cookery and as a feature of sweets, including:

1. Relative simplicity of basic recipe.

2. Ease of preparation yet with a call for some small skills in tossing and turning which tend to appeal to the chef as well as to his patron.

3. Scope for varying the ingredients in the basic mixture and the possibility of incorporating and adding ingredients and flavourings in the mixture itself.

4. Ability to take a wide range of garnish and fillings within the completed pancake.

5. Its capability of being pre-prepared (though desirably not too long in advance) for completion within the room.

6. Like most sweet flambé dishes the smell in cooking is agreeable.

7. The universal appeal of basic ingredients which are not sophisticated.

Crêpes Suzette

Unlike pêche Melba which has always been attributed without challenge to Escoffier, there has, in Britain at least, been some controversy about the creation and the creator of crêpe Suzette, the forerunner of so many flambé-d pancake dishes.

The man who claimed the credit for it and whose name has chiefly been associated with it was Henri Charpentier who died on Christmas Eve, 1961 at 81 years of age. The *New York Times* (he died in America where he had worked for most of his life) described him as a chef, but his own autobiography published in 1934, whilst indicating some early kitchen training, reveals him more as a restaurateur with experience predominantly on the waiting side and he did, indeed, claim to have invented crêpe Suzette by accident when working in 1894 as a fourteen-year-old commis de rang at Monte Carlo's Café de Paris.

According to his own story, Charpentier had not only taken charge of a table at which the then Prince of Wales (later Edward VII) was lunching with an unknown lady but had seized the opportunity to invent a new pancake dish, though the setting on fire of the liqueurs was inadvertent, hence the "accident" of its birth. Charpentier gave several details of the occasion, even of the clothes the prince was wearing, and the anecdote, indeed, occupies a whole chapter in his reminiscences. It records even Edward's desire to have the dish named not crêpe princesse, Charpentier's original suggestion for the pancake's title, but Suzette after his fair companion.

Yet many hoteliers on considering the anecdote have felt it strange that a fourteen-year-old commis should have been allowed to dance in attendance on this royal figure unsupervised. Equally strange that, in his book, Henri records addressing him as His Majesty thus anticipating Queen Victoria's death by half a dozen years. Despite the uneasiness of caterers, however, no documentary evidence to suggest other origins for crêpe Suzette's invention has yet emerged, though Marcel Boulestin recalled that the dish was served at the turn of the century in Paillards, one of the soigné restaurants in Paris at the corner of the Boulevard d'Italiens, and which the same Prince of Wales regularly patronised.

Tantalisingly, Boulestin does not record how crêpe Suzette came to be there and how it was then made.

The New York Times, in his obituary notice, described M. Charpentier, who was born in Nice, as a cousin of Auguste Escoffier and also a student of that famed chef. The journal recorded that Charpentier towards the end of his career operated one of the world's most unusual restaurants in his own home at Rodondo Beach, California, where his dining room held twelve, or sometimes sixteen people but no more: clients, it was said, made reservations four years in advance. Dinners taking all day to prepare and four hours to consume, at about 50s. a head, were accompanied by the aged restaurateur seated in a nearby rocking chair regaling diners with his reminiscences. Many must have swallowed his highly flavoured tales as easily as his crêpe Suzette—though possibly some of them found both a trifle indigestible.

Below is given a frequently encountered manner of preparing crêpe Suzette; though many maîtres d'hôtel, have, and will doubtless continue to add, their own personal touches. First the basic pancake mixture for kitchen use:

APPAREIL À CRÊPE—PANCAKE BATTER

½ lb. flour	1 tablesp. huile d'arachide (or
4–6 egg yolks	melted butter)
1 heaped tablesp. caster sugar	1 pint milk approx. *or*
1 level teasp. salt	¾ pint milk and ¼ pint cream

Method:

    1. Sieve together flour and salt and make a well or bay in the centre.

    2. Mix in the yolks diluting with a little milk gradually.

    3. Continuing to whisk, beat in remaining milk as necessary. The consistency should be of flowing, fresh cream.

    4. Leave until required, then stir in oil before use, re-stirring as batter is used.

To cook pancakes (in the kitchen, normally):

    1. Use iron crêpe pan exclusively reserved for such work, and wiped, *not* washed, for cleanliness.

    2. Use minimum oil or butter (clarified, unsalted butter is essential)—pour away from the hot pan any excess before adding the batter; alternatively add the oil to pan with brush or swab.

    3. Ensure the pan (and butter) is really hot.

    4. Use minimum batter—not much more than a table-spoonful is usually needed in the average crêpe pan. Twirl pan to spread the batter.

    5. Cook each side for about ½ to ¾ minute. Toss (or turn with palette knife) when first side is cooked.

There are many "favourite" recipes for crêpe batters but generally fine ones contain yolks and *not* the white of eggs and a little sweet oil or melted butter to ensure a pleasant, soft and pliant texture when cooked.

To make Crêpe Suzette

Despite the variations which have been introduced into a crêpe Suzette finished at the guéridon, the following items for mise en place are normally assembled and should be to hand in the sequence of use as follows:

Mise en place: Lamp and crêpe Suzette pan; service spoons and forks; hot plates; hot, cooked, thin, small pancakes from the kitchen (it is additionally desirable to have a rechaud or hot-plate to keep warm the plates and prepared pancakes); dish of butter; strainer (and possibly squeezer) for orange and lemon juice. Caster sugar and lump sugar (previously impregnated with aromatic oils from the orange zest), curaçao, cognac.

Note: In the preparation of crêpe Suzette it is customary to incorporate in the sauce the aromatic flavour from the orange zest (and even also from the lemon zest). This is achieved by rubbing lump sugar against the skin of a whole orange and this must be effected without fingering the orange once it is wiped, and without fingering the cube sugar. Hold the orange within a fold of a freshly laundered napkin and in the other hand hold the sugar in sugar tongs. This step is frequently taken in advance of service time.

Quantities for two covers:

2 oranges	1 measure cognac
1 lemon	3 oz. butter
6 lumps sugar	Caster sugar (about 2 oz.)
$\frac{1}{2}$ measure curaçao	

Method:

1. Arrange the mise en place neatly and in sequence on the guéridon.

2. Over a steady, medium flame heat a tablespoon of caster sugar and as it just begins to caramelise add an equal quantity of butter, blending thoroughly.

3. Add half the orange and lemon juice gradually, mixing thoroughly.

4. Dissolve the zest-impregnated lump sugar in the mixture.

5. Add the curaçao and reduce the flame.

6. Over a low flame lay in the pancakes one at a time. Coat them thoroughly and fold into triangles by two folds and place to the side of the pan as further crêpes are introduced.

7. During or after this process adjust the consistency of sauce with the remaining juice as necessary.

8. Arrange pancakes centrally in the pan, turn up the flame, tilt the pan slightly forward, add cognac to front of pan and flame.

9. Turn each pancake whilst the sauce flames. Serve immediately on to hotplates.

Inevitably, even this sort of "bespoke" item can now be obtained "off the peg" as it were. In U.S.A. is marketed a prepared crêpe Suzette batter mix. Obtainable too in Britain is a canned version, complete with sauce. Some operators use canned juice or canned frozen juice as a short cut. Most guests expect that in a restaurant this juice will be an individually and freshly made "bespoke" item.

HIGHLAND MARY'S PANCAKE

This adaptation of crêpe Suzette is a forgivable plagiarisation north of the border. Prepare as for Suzette with the following differences:

1. For the sauce, melt 1 oz. butter and instead of sugar blend in 2 tablespoons Scotch jelly marmalade (1 tablespoon orange jelly and 1 tablespoon lemon jelly marmalade).

2. In lieu of curaçao use 3 parts curaçao and 1 part Drambuie.

3. Substitute whisky for cognac.

Add liqueurs, lay in pancakes, coat with sauce and flambé in Suzette style.

For further variants in the British idiom, thought may be given to a crêpe sauce of golden syrup, lemon and cinnamon with Drambuie, Glayva or Morella cherry brandy. For "native fillings", Devon clotted cream with or without additions (such as strawberries) should be tried. Unfortunately honey is not too successful in table cooking as its smell when heated is not always agreeable and there is a general tendency to sickliness.

Further Pancakes

Crêpes are, of course, especially appropriate for service on Shrove Tuesday or Mardi-gras and one might well designate a house speciality, *Crêpe Maison flambée pour mardi-gras.*

The following pancake dishes may also be flambé-d.

CRÊPE À LA CONFITURE

Any jam may be used for pancake filling. After spreading, the pancake may be folded and rolled. Sent into the room after they have been sugar sprinkled and "flashed" under the salamander they may be flared at the moment of service with an appropriate liqueur. Possibilities are black cherry jam filling, flamed with kirsch, apple jelly flamed with calvados and so on.

CRÊPE NORMANDE

Filled with an apple purée (marmalade de pomme) these may be treated in similar style as *Crêpe à la confiture*.

CRÊPE AUX FRAISES (OR FRAMBOISES)

Strawberries (or raspberries) sugared and crushed, plain or blended with whipped cream may be used as a pancake filling.

Other Crêpe Fillings

Many fruits may be chopped or crushed for use as pancake fillings including pineapple, apricot, peach, mango and purées of blackcurrants, gooseberries and similar soft fruits.

Pistachio nuts, walnuts, crushed toasted almonds, introduced into crème Chantilly also gives an interesting crêpe fourré and marrons (including crème de marrons) are often used.

Fruit flavoured liqueurs of all kinds may be tried and matched to the fillings.

Crêpes Surprises

Skilful restaurateurs often feature "surprise" crêpes; that is pancakes with an ice cream filling and flamed. For this operation the crêpes themselves should be allowed to cool. Wrap the ice cream within the crêpe on a cold plate and then immerse all the filled crêpes so prepared at once in the hot sauce, add the chosen liqueur or spirit and flame immediately.

Mr Berti, restaurant manager of the Piccadilly restaurant celebrated for his touch with flambé dishes has a reputation for such a "hot and cold" item.

Crêpe Bannerman was a surprise speciality of this kind at Taglionis in Gerrard Street in the 1920's. The sauce was an adaptation of Suzette and the dish was named for the popular actress of that time, Miss Margaret Bannerman. The pancake filling of vanilla ice was further garnished with grated chocolate and nuts.

Names for Crêpes

In devising variants of pancake flambé dishes and in finding appropriate names for them inspiration may be aided by remembering how these are featured in many regions at home and abroad. There is even a pancake named Inverurie in which Scots' cooks introduce fine oatmeal into boiling milk and cool before completing the batter. This mix is later flavoured with nutmeg and lemon rind.

The lace-like, thin crêpes Bretonne have relatives all over France, and in the Auvergne pancakes have names like Sauciaux, Flognarde and Tourton. Batter with buttermilk and bicarbonate of soda yields Welsh pancakes named Campog whilst the Flenjes of Holland have a sophisticated version titled Flenjes Dorlas which is close kin to a crêpe Suzette.

A pannequet has been described as "a soufflé wrapped in a thin pancake",* though in France the term is used as an alternative to crêpe but usually implying that the pancake is rolled (normally with a sweet filling and sugared). Pannequets are ordinarily prepared in the kitchen but, sent promptly to the dining room, are well suited for flambé treatment.

Savoury Pancakes

Such is the versatility of the pancake that many interesting savoury items can be introduced as a pancake filling. Pancakes of this kind are not particularly suitable for flaring but, maybe, an ingenious maître d'hôtel might do something with items such as *Crêpe delices de la mer* or a *Crêpe de homard flambé à l'armagnac*.

OMELETTES

OMELETTE SOUFFLÉE FLAMBÉE

4 egg yolks	2 tablesp. sugar (preferably impregnated with vanilla pod)
1 oz. butter	
Liqueur gl. Drambuie and whisky in equal parts	6 egg whites

* James Beard and Alexander Watt, *Paris Cuisine*, McGibbon and Kee, 1953.

In the kitchen:

1. Beat together the yolks and sugar and if the sugar has not been stoppered with vanilla pod, flavour with a few drops of vanilla essence.

2. Separately beat the whites stiff and fold into the beaten yolks.

3. Pour the mixture into a buttered and sugared dariole mould and bake in a hot oven (425° F.) for a quarter of an hour or until the omelette is set and golden brown.

In the room:

1. Sprinkle the omelette with caster sugar.

2. In a warm ladle ignite a blend of Drambuie and whisky and pour over the omelette.

Variants: Heather honey may be substituted for the sugar in the omelette mixture (though use honey with caution as the bouquet and flavour can easily upset the balance of a dish). Of course, a dash of Drambuie in the omelette soufflé mix itself is a desirable addition.

OMELETTE DRAMBUIE

1 × 3 egg omelette (made in the kitchen)	1 tablesp. Drambuie
2 tablesp. Scotch whisky	Caster sugar

Method:

1. Make 3 or 4 light slits across the freshly made omelette.

2. Sprinkle with sugar and with a mixture of the Drambuie and half the whisky.

3. Immediately ignite the remaining whisky and pour over.

Omelettes, may, of course, be flamed with other liqueurs and jam omelettes as well as plain sweet ones may be so treated. Rum omelette is a popular, standard feature.

Savoury Omelettes

As in the case of crêpes, omelettes may also be *fourrées* (stuffed) with savoury fillings and flamed. Typical of this style is *Omelette flambée aux crevettes*, for which shrimps are blended in a creamy sauce to provide the filling and the omelette flamed, on comple-

Monkey Gland

A preliminary stage in the preparation of this flambé steak dish. The flattened fillet steak has been salt and pepper seasoned and is now being spread with moutarde forte de Dijon. Note amongst the mise en place: chopped shallot (or onion), parsley, butter, Worcestershire sauce, pepper mill and Hennessy's Bras Armé cognac for the final flaming.

Monkey Gland

With the chopped shallots already cooking in the butter, the maître d'hôtel lays in the seasoned and prepared steak.

Making Crêpes Suzette

The author demonstrates the preliminary impregnation of sugar lumps with the aromatic oil from orange zest. This is sometimes effected earlier than service time and "behind the scenes". When performed before the guest, the fruit must be held by and guarded with the napkin and the sugar lump held in tongs, thus avoiding finger contact. Gentle rubbing against the rind soon colours the sugar and gives it the flavour and perfume required. The same technique naturally applies to lemons, which most maîtres d'hôtel use in addition to oranges to give added piquancy.

First stage in making the sauce for crêpes Suzette. Over a steady flame the sugar melting and just turning pale gold now has butter added.

To the caramelized butter and sugar (including the zest flavoured lump) has been added orange and lemon juice and curaçao to form the Suzette sauce. Now the maître d'hôtel lays in the first crêpe which must be thoroughly "bathed" in the sauce.

Each pancake when well coated is folded twice to make a triangle.

This view of the blazer shows four folded pancakes in the sauce.

Now is added Hennessy cognac. Normally this is best pre-measured in a sauceboat for accuracy and safety.

With the cognac just added, the pan has been tilted to catch the flame and the crêpes are ablaze.

Bananes Flambées

Peeling and preparing bananas in the room: Method 1. In this method after severing the stem stump with a knife the skin is peeled away in the customary manner, *but* with a clean napkin, ensuring that the hands do not contact the fruit.

Peeling and preparing bananas in the room: Method 2. In this alternative method the banana has first been cut in half lengthwise. The waiter may now lift away the half banana with the knife point as pictured.

(*Left*) The first cooking step in banana flambé is to sauter in butter

(*Above*) During sauté-ing, sugar is added from the sifter and the caramelizing butter and sugar mix is basted over the bananas.

(*Left*) The third and final cooking step in banana flambé is the addition of rum and the tilting of the pan to catch the flame. It is usually better to measure the required quantity of rum into a sauceboat rather than to use the bottle; both because of accuracy in portioning and also so as not to expose the full bottle to the flame.

tion, with a light rum. Whilst this type of dish may be flared at the guéridon, it is apparent that savoury omelettes flambées are not obvious choices for ease of side-table work.

FRUITS

BANANES FLAMBÉS AU RHUM

| 3 bananas | 2 oz. caster sugar |
| 2 oz. butter | 1 measure rum |

To prepare the bananas: In order to save time, bananas are sometimes sent in from the kitchen peeled but where these are prepared at the table it is essential that they are treated in such a way as to be untouched by the waiter's hands. There are two main ways of preparing the banana at the side table:

1. Holding the banana with a napkin partially sever the top stalk end and peel in the conventional way by stripping down.

2. Probably the more usual way for guéridon treatment is to sever the banana into two halves lengthwise, using a sharpened knife. Then with service spoon and fork (or knife and fork if desired) gently ease away the skin edge and lift out the banana halves.

To prepare and cook the dish:
Method:

1. Melt the butter and when hot, sauté the banana quickly on both sides.

2. Continuing to heat, sprinkle over caster sugar, turning the banana.

3. As caramelisation begins add the rum and flare.

Alternative method:

Even with firm bananas there is sometimes a tendency for them to break up. An alternative mode is to heat the butter and sugar together, laying the halved bananas at an early stage of caramelisation. Over gentle heat turn the bananas to become thoroughly coated with the blend and well heated through. Flambé-ing is effected when this heating and basting have been achieved.

In the Chalet Restaurant in San Juan, Puerto Rico, where banana flambé flared with cognac is a dessert speciality it is accompanied by a cool sherbet.

CARRIBEAN BANANA

4 bananas   1 glass Bacardi rum
Juice of 1 orange   2 dessertsp. caster sugar
2 oz. butter   1 glass cointreau
Juice of ¼ lemon

Method:

1. Over steady flame, melt the butter and place in the peeled bananas.
2. Whilst slightly shaking the pan, turning the bananas, add the sugar, continuing to heat until caramelisation starts.
3. Add the fruit juice, continuing to apply the heat so that the liquid is well reduced as the bananas cook.
4. Add the cointreau, turning and basting the bananas thoroughly.
5. With the flame high, add the rum and flame. Serve immediately.

Note: Serving with praliné ice cream and adding flaked almonds to the sauce are additional service possibilities.

ORCHARD FIRE

In the kitchen: Poach peeled and cored apples in syrup and whilst still warm drain and fill with raisins and sultanas (plumped by macerating in Demarara sugar and rum). Send in a timbale to the room with the poaching liquor in a sauceboat.

In the room: Reduce the poaching liquor in the blazer over a high flame whilst stirring in a spoonful of apricot jam or sieved apricot pulp. Mask the apples with this sauce. In a warm ladle, flame a measure of cognac, rum, whisky or calvados and add.

Pears (or peaches) are capable of similar treatment with variable fillings including marrons, crèmes (with garnishing such as nuts or crystallised fruits).

FRUITS DE JUNGLE

Pineapple, preferably fresh but practicable even when canned, are useful for flambé purposes. Fresh pineapple is improved by maceration in sugar prior to cooking. An example of a treatment of pineapple is afforded by that at Glasgow's Boulevard Hotel where Mr George Mulvey presents *Fruits de jungle* by sauté-ing pineapple rings in butter, forming a caramel by adding brown sugar and flaming with Tia Maria. He serves this with coffee ice cream garnished with chopped walnuts.

Fruits and Butter in the Blazer

Some consider butter and pineapple incompatible and certainly this fruit (and also pears) do not seem to take too kindly to pan frying in butter. Generally, heating such fruits in a little poaching syrup prior to flambé-ing is preferable. If butter is used, take the minimum necessary.

COMPÔTES PANACHÉES AU KIRSCH

Biscuit glacé aux fraises (whole, small strawberries)	Blackcurrants
	Red currants
Raspberries	Half peaches

In the kitchen:

All fruit should be appropriately cooked in syrup flavoured with maraschino and sent to the dining room in silver timbales (hot) accompanied by friandises, demi-sec biscuits, kirsch and sugar.

In the room:

1. Warm the blazer over the lamp and rub with clean serviette.
2. Place heaped dessertspoonful of each of the soft fruits alternately round the pan leaving the centre for the peaches.
3. Sprinkle sugar over the fruit and heat gently.
4. When it is hot enough, place a wine glass full of kirsch over and flame it at the moment when the biscuit glacé has been presented and a portion served to each guest.
5. Serve each guest a portion of each fruit with the ice.

Accompaniments: Place friandises and demi-secs on the table.

Cérises Jubilee

This dish has been so adapted and elaborated that it is difficult to define what may now be accepted as a pure or "classic" *Cérises Jubilee*.

Escoffier's method in the early years of this century was to thicken with arrowroot the syrup in which cherries had been poached (1 tablespoon arrowroot per ½ pint), dish into individual timbales, top with a coffeespoonful of kirsch and ignite. The much admired chef pâtissier Kollist stressed the need to thicken the syrup (with either arrowroot or cornflour) so that the kirsch topping will not too readily combine with the mix and may readily flare.

Deviations include napping with Melba sauce before flaming. Some sprinkle poached cherries with sugar before adding kirsch and flaring whilst others have combined red currant jelly with the poaching liquor to form a sauce. Cherries Jubilee are always served hot but nowadays they are sometimes accompanied by vanilla ice cream or are spooned, flaming, over the vanilla ice cream.

Poached Fruits Flared

Many fruits when simply poached can be flamed to make successful, simple sweets. Especially suitable are choice items such as comice pears (for example, *Doyen de comice fourré aux marrons*) flambé in kirsch and fine, soft fruits in season. This also includes canned fruits particularly, perhaps, green figs, passion fruit, whole peaches and even eastern and exotic items such as lichees, paw paw and mango pieces. Fruit salad also may be featured as, for example, *Macédoine de fruits flambée au kirsch*.

It is usually advisable to lié fruit syrup with cornflour to prevent too quick absorption of the flambé-ing liqueur. Spooning over already flaming liqueur from a warm ladle is also a reliable method.

A simple but effective pêche flambée may be achieved by filling the cavity of a half peach with warm cognac and igniting. Other fruits and other liqueurs may be similarly treated.

OTHER SWEETS

Tartelettes flambées

Warm fruit flans, particularly individual tartelettes make simple but effective flambé services. Cherry, strawberry, pineapple, apple, peach and other fruits placed in "blind" baked tartelette or flan cases, then glazed will take flaming either by pouring over a little spirit—cognac, whisky, calvados, light rum and so on, or by spooning over liqueur already flaming from a warmed ladle.

Effective naming may be possible by borrowing from French regional sources such as Clafoutis, fruit tart normally cherry; Milard, cherry tart; Flamousse, apple tart featured in Berry and Auvergne.

Puddings Flared

It should not be forgotten that one most distinctively British speciality, the plum pudding or Christmas pudding, has been served flambé for many, many years. Rum, whisky and brandy are suitable for this.

Snapdragon—flamed Christmas fruits such as muscatels and sultanas (and sometimes nuts) to tease the fingers—has also been a festive table frivolity for a long time.

Basic meringue mixture poached in spoonfuls then flamed in whisky makes fine flaming "Highland Snow" to top a mountainous pudding.

Flaming, can, therefore, certainly be claimed as a process just as British as foreign. We can experiment with flaming other puddings and sweets still in our own tradition. A spooning of flaming whisky over crème brulé, for example, or over latticed minced tarts and even more adventurous treatment of individual sized steamed puddings other than Christmas ones may evoke even further thoughts and possibilities.

CHAPTER 7

CARVING IN THE RESTAURANT

Because carving is not only an important but also a relatively extensive activity in food service, it is once again important to define the scope of this chapter.

Carving in the restaurant inevitably differs from carving within the kitchen itself and this is largely because the emphasis within the restaurant is not only on making an effective presentation. At the same time carving must be accomplished with dexterity and speed so as to avoid the cooling of hot items under the guest's eye and scrupulous attention must be paid to the appearance of all the implements and equipment used.

Carving within the kitchen must also, of course, be a hygienic and properly accomplished process. Moreover, even in "behind the scenes" carving the emphasis is on the appearance of resultant portions on the serving dish and on the plate. The chief differences lie, perhaps, in that (1) kitchen carving allows greater latitude in the choice of tools and that (2) especially for such table d'hôte items as roast fowl, techniques may be applied in the kitchen which are quite unsuitable within the room itself, for example, the chopping through of bones.

Chef Trancheur

Where the carving of small items, such as châteaubriands, côte à l'os and entrecôte double are concerned the portioning aspect of carving diminishes in importance since it is relatively simple. Where large joints such as roasts of beef and cold hams are concerned, then the skills needed are not merely clean cutting and dexterity but the ability to gauge accurate portions visually. Such

92

carving of larger items may take place either within the kitchen, at a buffet or from carving wagons or trolleys within the room itself. But generally speaking these larger joints remain the responsibility of the chef and his staff. In substantial operations a large kitchen brigade will normally include a chef trancheur and whether the skills of this specialist are exercised within the restaurant itself from a voiture or buffet table or from the servery or garde manger within the kitchen the techniques employed remain substantially the same.

Waiter as Carver

Many of the best waiters, particularly in pre-war times and certainly many of those promoted to maître d'hôtel, have prided themselves on preliminary kitchen training before going into the restaurant to learn waiting. At one time a senior waiter might well have been capable of most general carving. Even today for some types of first class service there remains a case for the waiter's skills to be based on an introductory kitchen spell. A little preliminary kitchen work for waiters should include especially such work as will increase understanding of the meat, fish, poultry and game carved in the room.

In the main this chapter is chiefly concerned with those smaller items of poultry, meat and fish which have almost been devised with their carving and service from the guéridon as an integral part of the presentation. In good class à la carte services this type of guéridon work has always been of importance. Carving remains an area of activity which underscores the skills of the waiter and reveals his work to be one for which training and flair are required.

Carving Equipment

The carving knives used for large joints include special, long, thin bladed knives of either French or English style together with special double-tined forks with or without protective guards. Such tools are, however, in the restaurant business regarded largely as chefs' implements.

A waiter will rely chiefly upon his ordinary "service gear" from the sideboard mise en place to effect the greater part of his carving work. Clearly the prudent waiter often reserves a table knife to which he imparts an especially keen edge in order to deal with double steaks or carré d'agneau; but it would certainly not be within restaurant tradition to use kitchen or carving knives for such purposes.

Even carving equipment of domestic pattern and such as would be used from the sideboard of a private home are seldom encountered in restaurant carving, except possibly from the carving voiture or from a buffet side table. The question of special equipment for cutting or of a special fork does not really arise; nor do professional waiting staffs have recourse to such devices as poultry secateurs and so on. Unless otherwise indicated, therefore, it may be assumed that for the carving process described in the notes which follow, all that is required are well sharpened table knives and forks. A carborundum or the gadget incorporating twin carborundum wheels is useful in ensuring a keen edge on such implements.

When carving, allow the knife to move freely backwards and forwards, cutting through lightly with a sawing action. Excessive pressure results in squeezing out too much juice, misshapen meat and often displacement of material from plate to table cloth should the knife slip. Blunt knives inducing heavy cutting pressure are more frequent accident causers than good keen blades.

Carving from the Trolley

In the case of joints carved at the trolley conventional carving tools are customarily used, in particular the carving knife and the longer and thinner bladed carving knife which is also suitable for legs of pork and similar joints. The carving fork, with appropriate "guard" is also required but for some joints (for example the leg of lamb and shoulder) the trimmed bone may be held manually providing the hand is covered with a perfectly clean napkin (or ham frill fixed on). Certainly beef, pork and ham are cut thinly (except for loin of pork). Lamb, mutton and veal may be cut in rather thicker slices.

The equipment chapter has mentioned trolleys available and also the heated table carving stand which fulfils a similar though static function. Suffice to emphasise here that trolley mise en place should be fully incorporated into the ménage drill before service. Trolleys should be checked for adequate supply of warmed plates; appropriate garnish in the sauce and other receptacles; lamps filled and wicks trimmed, thoroughly cleaned, lit and ready in advance of the room opening. Similarly at the close of service, the carving trolley should be disconnected (lamps extinguished) and thoroughly cleaned without delay.

Fish are sent into the restaurant in various cuts and styles. They may, for example, be whole or portioned (with bone) into cuts like steaks or tronçons. Frequently they are boned prior to cooking and sent for service as fillets or cuts of fillets. Filleted portions do not as a rule require any further trimming or attention from the guéridon.

Occasionally dishes of fish dressed with sauce may be filleted at the table, for example, a whole sole Mornay. As this is difficult to do without spoiling the dressing and appearance, fish carving normally and chiefly applies to fish that have been subjected to plain poaching, grilling and shallow frying. Otherwise fish dishes carefully dressed by the chef in the kitchen normally have their filleted portions pre-prepared so that the décor does not have to be deranged by the mode of service.

Larger fish, such as salmon or turbot, when presented whole, are normally carved from the buffet table though it is just possible that this may be done from a serving wagon by the guests' table.

Carving of fish undertaken by the maître d'hôtel and his staff is largely the filleting of smaller ones (particularly sole) and skin trimming and bone removal in the case of salmon steaks and tronçons or of other fish such as turbot, halibut and so on.

Some small fish cooked and presented whole are not truly "carved" or filleted but the head and tail need to be removed; normally the waiter will do this, using a service spoon and fork. Examples of such fish are herrings, trout, whiting, mackerel.

Sole

Sole is, perhaps, the fish most frequently portioned by waiters on the side table. There are at least three different techniques for "carving" or filleting a cooked sole at the guéridon, and methods of removing the bone hinge upon the preceding mode of cooking or dressing the fish. These may be grouped as follows:

Sole, Method I

Especially when sole has been poached and dressed or napped with sauce (i.e. Mornay or bonne femme) proceed as follows:

1. Lift the sole from the silver on to a large joint plate.
2. Trim as necessary the head and tail (side or "wing" bones are normally removed prior to cooking when sole is sauce coated).
3. Ease one of the forks gently under the skin and run the fork down the backbone from head to tail, loosening the two bottom fillets.
4. Repeat the procedure, loosening the two top fillets.
5. With one fork holding the fillets in place, lift with the other fork the complete bone out of the side of the sole.
6. Replace the sole, minus the bone, back on the silver, re-garnish and serve.

This technique is adopted so as to disturb as little as possible the chef's dressing of the fish.

Sole, Method II (for use especially when Grilled, Fried or Meunière)

1. Using two service forks, lift the sole from the silver flat on to a large joint plate.
2. Then remove the head, tail and side (or "wing") bones.
3. Using two forks, press the prongs down through each side of the backbone and gently ease the top and bottom fillets together from the backbone. Ease from head to tail until the bone is completely clear of the fillets.
4. Now lift the bone away.
5. Reform the fillets together again and lift back the sole on to the silver.

Sole Colbert

In the kitchen, the raw sole has been treated as follows:

After slight trimming of fin and tail bone the flesh is detached and rolled away from each side of the central spine bone. This is done on one side only and reveals a substantial area of bone which is then broken.

The whole fish is pané-d (egg and breadcrumbed) and deep fried.

In the room, therefore, the waiter completes the procedure in the following way:

1. Removes head and completes any necessary trimming away of tail and side bones.

2. Lifts out the broken spine bone in one piece. As the fillets have been "rolled back" by the preliminary kitchen treatment, it is fairly simple to discover and extract this backbone (despite its breadcrumb coating) with two forks, gently easing out.

3. Returns the fish to silver flat on réchaud, places maître d'hôtel butter in the cavity left by the bone's removal and serves.

In all the foregoing treatments of sole, most waiters find two forks the best combination of implements, certainly for transferring back the boned fish to the silver flat. There are some, however, who employ a fish knife and fork, and even service spoon and fork. There is no reason to be didactic about the best tools; and those which give the individual operator the best results may be regarded as the best for him.

Fish Tronçons and Cutlets

For tronçons, cutlets and steaks of the larger, round white fish such as cod, fresh haddock, halibut and similar types the following is customary.

Remove the outside skin and centre bone. Skin may be effectively detached by securing one end with a fork and thereafter twisting the fork so that the skin curls around the fork prongs as it is removed from around the fish cutlet. The skin normally comes away quite cleanly but may be eased as necessary with a spoon held in the other hand. Skinning is usually effected with service spoon and fork but some operators may wish to employ a fish knife and fork. Once the skin is away the centre bone is then removed.

For cuts of the large flat white fish such as turbot and brill, the skin and wing bones may be removed, indeed, the flesh removed from the bone entirely. Some guests are, however, partial to the gelatinous side bones of, for example, turbot and treatment will be affected by their wishes.

Whole Turbot and Brill

Begin to carve the white skinned side as this is obviously preferred to the back flesh which is covered with the blacker skin.

Cut along the middle of the fish from head to tail. Then outline, with the point of the knife, lines at right angles so as to form portions about 2 ins. wide.

Whole Salmon

Strip away the skin from head to tail. Make an incision along the middle of the fish from head to tail, halving it along its backbone. Carve away portions at right angles from the side of the fish at about 1½–2 ins. in width.

Trout, Small Whiting, Red Mullet, Mackerel, Herring, etc.

When quite small this type of fish may be served whole, but normally the guest is asked whether he wishes the head and tail removed (with service spoon and fork) at the side table.

POULTRY AND GAME

Roast Chicken

Have ready sharpened a table knife and table fork and also a large, warmed plate. Allow the jus or gravy to drain away from inside the chicken into the gravy boat by lifting and tilting it over the silver flat when transferring the bird from the silver dish to the heated plate on which the carving should be done. Then:

> 1. With the bird upright outline with the top of the knife the cut for later removal of the wings.
> 2. Turn the bird on to its side and remove the leg followed by the wing.
> 3. Reverse the bird and repeat the operation.
> 4. Finally, with the bird on its breast, remove the wishbone section.
> 5. In serving, the legs can be severed to form two portions and the drumstick so yielded can either augment the wishbone or be reserved for second servings.

As portions are removed from the chicken they may be transferred to the silver flat for passing to the guests or portioned directly on to guests' plates. For side-table carving in this style, bones should be severed through only at connecting joint and never chopped through.

Poussin and Pigeon
Serve these whole or halved lengthwise.

Chicken Spatchcock
For chicken spatchcock the bird is opened in the kitchen by severing through the backbone, legs pinioned to the carcase so that a flat piece for grilling is obtained.

In the room, the bird is divided into two by cutting hard through the breast bone. Usually halving suffices (for only small young birds are used) but if required legs may be detached as previously outlined.

Crapaudine is simply a spatchcock chicken with "eyes" of truffle, egg white (or similar) placed to simulate a toad or frog appearance. Portioning is the same.

Pheasant
Normally, in the restaurant, pheasant is carved for the breast only in the manner outlined for duck (below). As the breast inclines to dryness fewer and slightly thicker slices usually result. (For table d'hôte use, pheasant may be kitchen carved as for a chicken.)

Duck
1. Have ready a sharpened table knife and table fork together with the warmed large dinner plate.

2. Drain jus from interior of the duck into the sauceboat of gravy or on to the silver flat or service dish whilst transferring the bird to the plate on which carving correctly is done.

3. Loosen the legs and press them back and away from the sides but, as the legs are not generally served in the highest class of restaurant operation, it is not necessary to sever them.

4. Carve thin slices from each side of the breast bone so as to gain at least four slices from each side.

Note the difference in the above procedure for high class guéridon carving and the following kitchen method suitable for table d'hôte work:

With the duck on its side, remove the leg by inserting the fork into the leg joint and gently lifting upwards. At the same time sever the surrounding meat from the carcase with the knife.

Similarly remove the wing, lifting with the fork in the bone joint, at the same time cutting with the knife against the carcase.

Remove the breast by severing with the knife pressing against the side of the breast bone and lifting gently away with the fork. Turn the bird and remove the same three portions from the reverse side.

Turkey

Cut around the leg with a knife and detach from the body in the same way as for chicken. The leg is halved by cutting through the joint and dark meat cut from each piece in slices. The wing is detached together with a little surrounding meat and either the meat cut from it or served whole in the case of smaller birds. Remove the breast in regular slices.

Partridge and Grouse

For small partridge remove the legs and serve the following three portions: the two wings detached as for chicken with little surrounding meat with the breast forming a third portion. Very small birds may be served whole or halved.

Wild Duck

Only the breast is for carving and serving. Indeed, only the flesh from the true breast end as distinct from the part towards the vent is succulent. Loosen legs and prepare as for reared ducks (above); then remove the breast in thin slices with a sharp knife in lines parallel to the breast bone.

STEAKS

The larger or double steaks to serve two persons are invariably carved by the waiter at the guéridon. Those principally encountered are noted below. Specialities such as planked steaks may be carved on the plank when they are double steaks of this kind.

Châteaubriand

According to Frank Schloesser (*The Greedy Book*, 1906), the double sized or extra large steak cut from the "head" or thick end of the fillet of beef was first presented at Champeaux Restaurant, Place de la Bourse in 1802. Because of the steak's large size it was then thought desirable, because the exterior might tend to over-cook, to "sandwich" it between two thinner slices of inferior cut. When grilling was over the outside pieces could be discarded. Why the name Châteaubriand? Because, records Schloesser, "the profane wits of the kitchen" thought that a good steak sent to the fire between two malefactor steaks was a fair parody of Château-briand's work *Le Genie du Christianisme* published during that period.

Today, the châteaubriand is normally a double fillet steak cut from the head or top of the fillet, i.e. the thickest end which passes through the sirloin into the rump. It is more frequently grilled (though it may be sauté au beurre) and it is sent to the table with an accompanying portion of grilled prime suet fat.

To carve châteaubriand:

1. Transfer from serving dish to warmed plate.
2. With sharpened table knife and fork trim as necessary (though most guests prefer to eat the entire portion enjoying the charred flavour of the exterior).
3. Using slanting cuts, slice into about 4 thick portions transferring these to the serving dish on the réchaud or hot-plate.
4. Cut the grilled suet and place one or two pieces per guest for service.
5. Cut the remainder of the suet and any steak trimmings. Squeeze them between two plates (take a second warmed plate) and pour the resultant jus over the dished, carved steak.

Alternatively, this extract may be blended with further jus rôti, French mustard, and/or sherry, seasoning and, perhaps, a dash of Worcestershire sauce for blending in the chafing dish to form a sauce (As also in the case of the entrecôte double and côte à l'os below.)

Porterhouse Steak

Porterhouse steak or "T" bone steak is prepared from the sirloin and includes both the undercut and the contrefilet. Thus it re-sembles a large loin chop. As when carving other large steaks, use a table knife and fork and transfer the meat to a warm plate.

Then to carve:

1. Secure the meat by inserting the fork in the tail and remove the undercut by cutting hard against the "T" bone.

2. Then similarly remove the contrefilet side.

3. Put away the bone.

4. Cut the undercut into two portions and replace them on serving dish.

5. Trim away excess fat from the contrefilet side and remove the inferior tail meat.

6. Carve the remaining contrefilet meat into four thick slices using a slanting cut and transfer to the serving dish.

7. Cut the trimmings and using a second warmed plate squeeze (as with châteaubriand débris above) and similarly use the extracted jus.

Côte à l'os—Rib steak on the bone

Côte à l'os is a steak cut from the prime rib part or forerib of beef. It is trimmed so that only the rib bone remains. The rib bone end is further trimmed so that the final cut resembles a large cutlet. As in the case of châteaubriands and entrecôtes doubles, côte à l'os is grilled, normally rather underdone and sent to the room on a silver flat. Carve with sharpened table knife and fork.

At the guéridon:

1. Transfer the côte à l'os to a warmed plate. Keep warm the silver dish.

2. Using a napkin take hold of the trimmed end of the bone and with a sharpened table knife cut off the bone. Do this by cutting closely to the bone. Set aside the bone.

2. Now trim away excess fat and the inferior meat from the "tail".

4. Carve the remaining centre portions in diagonal slices about one inch thick using a slanting cut. This should yield four or five slices for transfer to the silver flat.

5. Now cut the meat and fat trimmings into smaller pieces and using a second warmed plate, squeeze to extract the juice.

6. Add this plainly to the carved meat or blend into a sauce along the lines suggested for châteaubriand or entrecôte double.

Carving a Chicken

1. *Removing the leg.* The carver has used the table knife to detach the leg from the side of the carcase. He must now ease away by lifting firmly with the fork whilst continuing to sever with the knife any connecting flesh. The leg should come away quite cleanly.

2. *Removing the wing.* After cutting through a portion of the white meat of breast, the carver is now about to sever the cartilage where the wing bone joins the carcase.

Meat left on each side of the breast bone may be either (*a*) lifted away in one piece or (*b*) carved off independently from each side.

1. *Method I.* With one fork holding the sole steady, the carver has eased away the flesh first by inserting the fork below the bone. He follows by similarly removing the flesh from above the bone. He may now remove (as pictured) the complete bone by gentle withdrawal with the fork. The completed fish is returned to the silver flat on the réchaud for completion of service.

Filleting a Sole

2. *Method II.* The carver has removed head and tail fin bones (placed on side plate off picture). Now, with 2 forks, he clears fish away by gentle withdrawal along and from the central spine bone. When the bone has been completely revealed it is lifted away and the fish reformed. The whole fish, bonefree, is returned to the silver flat on the réchaud for service.

Filleting a Sole

3. *Method III.* Earlier, in the kitchen, the raw sole was prepared as follows:
1. Slight trimming of fin and tail bone. 2. Fish detached from each side of central spine bone on one side to reveal the bone which is then broken. 3. The fish is panéed and deep fried.

Thus in the room the carver has been able (as in the picture) to lift out the spine bone in one piece. It may sometimes be necessary to ease away the flesh a little further before this can be effected. Return fish to silver flat on réchaud, place maître d'hôtel butter in the cavity left by the bone's removal and serve.

Note: Some waiters prefer to trim off fat and tail meat first whilst holding the côte à l'os trimmed bone in the napkin (or with paper frill if this is adequate and dry).

Entrecôte double

A double entrecôte is a steak (normally about one inch thick) cut from the sirloin. It is customarily grilled to remain underdone.

For carving have ready:

1. Sharpened table knife and fork and warmed plate.

2. Transfer the steak from the silver flat to the plate then trim away excess fat and the ends and edges of the steak.

3. Carve the trimmed meat into slices about $1\frac{1}{2}$ ins. thick using a slanting cut. This should yield four thick portions.

4. Return the slices to the silver dish which is being kept hot on a chauf plat.

5. Using another warmed plate and with the ends and trimmings cut into manageable pieces squeeze this residue between the two plates. The resultant jus is squeezed over the carved portions.

As described for châteaubriands, the squeezed jus may be turned into sauce varied according to the restaurant's speciality. An example is:

French Mustard Sauce for Double Steaks

1. Heat the jus from squeezed steak débris augmented with a little jus lié (roast gravy) in the chafing dish.

2. Monter au beurre (drop in knobs of butter, agitating the pan), using about $\frac{1}{4}$ oz butter per cover.

3. Stir in a heaped French mustardspoon of Dijon mustard.

4. Complete the seasoning with salt and, possibly, a dash of Worcestershire or Soy sauce.

Plank Steak

Plank steak or planked steak is not a common presentation nowadays. It once had a vogue in America and even in France entrecôte à la planche is not unknown.

The chief work for its service is in the kitchen, where the hardwood "plank" (about the size of a small breadboard), usually of oak or teak, is kept well dressed and soaked with salad oil. The steak is partially grilled then "finished" on the plank in a sharp oven.

Some "planks" are grooved to capture the flow of juice from steaks such as côte à l'os or entrecôte double, which are carved at the guéridon. Others may be quite small for service direct to the guest, fitting into a silver container or within an underplate.

JOINTS OF MEAT

As already noted, larger joints are normally carved by the specialist trancheur. The best end or rack of lamb trimmed as a carré and with bone tips cleaned and frilled is, however, usually handled by the waiter at the guéridon. Carrés of mutton and veal and, even, pork may be similarly treated.

Carrés (of Lamb, Mutton, Pork and Veal)

For large carrés (pork and veal) it is necessary to cut alternate slices consisting of a cutlet with bone, followed by a cutlet slice without bone.

For the smaller carré of lamb it is, of course, perfectly possible and customary to divide simply into cutlets with bone.

The carré d'agneau (best end of lamb) must be properly chined before cooking. If this is done, cutting with sharpened table knife along the bone portions to remove the cutlets is not difficult.

Loins

Loins must be properly prepared by the butcher (or chef garde manger) and particularly the bones adequately jointed (just as the carré must be chined). Carving is as for carré but the resultant portions will have the appearance of loin chops rather than cutlets.

In the case of pork, not only should the chine bone be sawn through but the rind must be scored.

Larger joints even including those mentioned below are not often carved by waiters from the side table but as restaurant staff may occasionally need to assist at a buffet they are briefly noted.

Leg of Lamb or Mutton

Carve downwards removing slices at right angles to the leg bone. Some carvers take from the middle, subsequently carving alter-

nate slices outwards. Others begin towards the knuckle end. Fatty
portions may be carved diagonally from the flap of meat at the
aitch bone end.

Shoulder of Lamb or Mutton

Take a few slices from the knuckle end at right angles to the sharp
blade bone (as in the preliminary cuts when carving a leg) and
remove as many slices as is possible from this section until the
shoulder bone is encountered. Then cut at right angles from the
first cut taking slices from each side of the blade bone. When the
top of the shoulder is stripped by carving in this manner, turn the
joint over and carve remaining slices along its whole length.

Shoulder of lamb or mutton generally proves one of the most
difficult of joints for the carving novice and, as a guide for the
future, it is obviously helpful for the beginner to study the shape
of the blade bone when it is stripped.

Saddle of Lamb or Mutton

The saddle corresponds in lamb to the sirloin in beef except that
in lamb the joint is a double one. (The single joint is the loin mentioned above.) The undercut or filet mignon is simply sliced to
accompany the top cuts.

Normally, in the room, the best methods followed and sometimes called the French styles are either: (a) to carve long, vertical
slices parallel to the backbone from the centre outwards or (b)
similarly to carve long slices horizontally from each side towards
and at right angles to the backbone.

An alternative mode, considered more economical, often called
the English style, is to cut downwards at right angles to the spine
to give slices resembling (though thinner than) the *noisette* (or
boneless chop) cut.

Sirloin of Beef

The "T" bone should be pre-jointed so that the "T" bone flap on
the contrefilet side may be detached. Then the carving knife can
more easily detach or loosen the meat from the remaining bone.
This then facilitates the removal of long thin slices slightly diagonal
from the contrefilet side. The filet or undercut is normally removed by slicing somewhat *with* the grain giving diagonal slices.

When carving the fillet, it is important to remove the surrounding membrane or "skin" which, though thin, is tough.

Forerib of Beef

Carved in like manner to the contrefilet side of the sirloin.

Haunch of Venison

The haunch of venison consists simply of the loin and leg complete. It is possible also to have haunch of lamb, mutton or even pork; though nowadays these are less frequently encountered than venison. Carve a haunch as for the individual cuts of loin and leg of lamb.

Ham and Gammon

Ham and gammon are from the same part of the pig but the latter is trimmed off with a straight cut, whereas the ham takes a rounded portion of meat from the haunch or rump of the animal. The rounded ham shape is more customarily seen on buffet tables and carving wagons.

As for a leg of lamb and leg of pork, the ham is cut downwards at right angles to the bone with rather more diagonal cuts. Slices from the thicker and fleshier end should be alternated and portioned with slices from the knuckle end.

Underneath cuts are normally reserved for sandwiches or other secondary purposes (croquettes, etc.), but it is possible to use them to augment the top cuts.

The essence of carving a ham is to obtain slices as thinly cut as possible. Hence the need for a long, keen, thin-bladed knife.

CHAPTER 8

SOME SPECIALITIES AND THEIR SERVICE

There is such a wide range of dishes which are subject to special forms of service or which make special presentations in the restaurant that it would be beyond the scope of this manual to consider them all. Gastronomic factors in conjunction with those of merchandising and promotion, have long made something of a ceremony of the presentation of choice foods—particularly expensive ones. The price of caviar no less than its palatability underlines the need for a degree of ritual in offering it; and one could well classify the presentation of hot blinis on one plate and the service of chilled caviar with its various accompaniments on another as an opportunity for special service. Similar considerations apply to foie gras and terrines, to melons, snails and a host of other overture items.

In this chapter consideration may, perhaps, be better directed to items which typify rather than exhaust the resourcefulness and ingenuity of restaurateurs in heightening the appeal of their fare by visual and by service means. In the case of one or two specialities the degree of attention at the guéridon or at point of service may be slight, as is the case, for example, in the method of offering *Suprême de volaille sous cloche* which is, nevertheless, treated amongst the following notes. Such dishes are included because, though not involving a high degree of service skill at the side table, they none the less are examples of the dramatic touch in food presentations having customer appeal.

In contrast is another dish—*Canard à la presse*—which whilst by no means lacking customer appeal of this kind does involve, in the room itself, a degree of elaboration and of costly ingredients which determines that it must be an item sold at high price.

POULTRY AND GAME

Canard à la presse—Pressed Duck

Canard à la presse is inevitably associated with its "temple"—the Tour d'Argent in Paris and which has registered by numbering every duck so served since 1890. With its splendid view overlooking Notre Dame, the Tour d'Argent is today a charming as well as a famous restaurant. Its original proprietor, Frederic, exacting high priest of gastronomy associated with its earlier days and original form, has passed into legend. He was described by the Edwardian gastronomic writer Newnham Davis as "one of the most original and most accomplished" of the great maîtres d'hôtel but writing of Frederic and the Tour d'Argent some sixty years ago Newnham Davis did not even mention its now great dish, *Canard à la presse*.

For this operation, a dual one of cuisine and waiter service, a duck should rather be a duckling not above two months old but not less than six weeks and well fattened during the last fortnight. Ducks should, furthermore, be dispatched in Rouen style and strangled and suffocated so that there is no loss of blood. Newnham Davis asserts that "of course the Rouen is not any particular breed of duck, though the good people of Rouen will probably stone you if you assert this. It is simply a roan duck."

The dish co-ordinates effort in the kitchen and the room; for the birds must be roasted behind the scenes and a good stock (or jus rôti) prepared with the carcases of other ducks. The duck liver used in the sauce finishing is also preferably prepared in the kitchen.

Variously designated *Canard à la presse*, *Caneton rouennais à la presse*, *Rouennais à la presse*, *Canard au sang* or *Canard Frédéric* its accompaniment sanctified by the Tour d'Argent, is customarily soufflé-d potatoes.

To make *Canard à la presse*

Mise en place:

Duck press	Sharpened table knife and fork
Roast duck	for carving
Sauceboat of chopped liver	Service spoon and fork
Sauceboat of jus rôti	Réchaud
Additional silver flat	Lamp and blazer.
Brandy, Port, Burgundy	

In the kitchen: Roast a young duck briskly for approximately 20 minutes to half an hour but so that it is underdone. Send it to the room with its jus (gravy) in an accompanying sauceboat, together with its raw liver finely chopped.

In the room:

1. Remove the legs and reserve for future use (they are usually finished on the grill and served with tossed salad).

2. Carve the breast thinly and arrange on a warm silver flat.

3. Break up the carcase in the presse and extract the blood and juice. (Moisten as necessary with a little roast duck gravy and Burgundy for maximum extraction.)

4. Blend the chopped liver with 1 tablespoon brandy and 2 of port.

5. Heat the sauce on the lamp, blend in the liver mix continuing to heat without boiling and adding further roast gravy as necessary.

6. Pour the completed sauce over the carved breast.

The sliced duck may also be flambé with brandy prior to adding the sauce.

Parfait of foie gras or good liver pâté may be substituted for duck liver.

Chicken in the Basket

The fried chicken of the "deep south" rather like well fried fish and chips in Britain, though having one of the simpler and less sophisticated flavours, has consistent appeal. Emphasising the simplicity of fried chicken as a contrast from the elaborations of, say, Chicken Maryland, has proved highly successful in the case of "chicken in the basket". This latter dish is indeed nothing more than it is said to be and consists of plainly deep-fried portions of jointed chicken (previously lightly dredged with seasoned flour), well drained after frying and presented in a small basket. This basket is normally the small round wicker type used to present bread and is lined with either paper napkins or preferably a linen napkin on which paper ones or paper d'oyleys are placed. The concept of "chicken in the basket" is to encourage the diner to shed inhibitions, to pick up the pieces and nibble away.

Service, therefore, presents few problems. Normal accompaniments may include salad with salad side plate and/or possibly baked, jacket potatoes also suitable for side plate service. Other vegetables if selected (and French fried potatoes often are) should not go in the basket but are also served separately plated. The nature of this dish makes finger bowls an essential accompaniment.

Chicken à la Kiev

This is a more sophisticated example of fried chicken in which the chief skills are in the kitchen. Sealing the butter filling within chicken suprêmes and subsequently frying so as to encase within the flesh a bubble, as it were, of hot butter requires dexterity and knowledge from the chef. Nevertheless, presentation at the table as, for example, in the old days at the Hungaria under the watcheye of the late Joseph Vecchi, gives the final touch to this dish. After simple serving from the guéridon and when the suprême is in front of the guest the waiter then suggests that he pierces the chicken morsel at the side and with the sharp point of a knife so as to release without disaster to the guest the confined hot butter —only too likely to squirt the unwary guest attempting to cut this himself for the first time.

SUPRÊME DE VOLAILLE SOUS CLOCHE

Suprêmes of chicken	Cream
Seasoned flour	Mushrooms
Oil	Sherry
Butter	

In the kitchen:

1. Remove the legs from a clean, drawn chicken by severing through the bone where it is jointed to the carcase and set aside the legs for alternative culinary use (for example, grilling, sautés, fricassés or currying).

2. Similarly remove the winglet.

3. Remove the skin by pulling away from the breast and cutting clear from the wings.

4. Trim away the flesh towards the wing tips so as to lay bare the bone (as is done in trimming cutlets). Chop the wing bone neatly leaving one inch of cleaned bone exposed.

5. Searching for the wishbone with the fingers, fillet it out

by using the point of a sharp knife. (The wishbone is, of course, at the neck end of the bird.)

6. Remove the fillets or suprêmes by cutting away with a filleting knife from against the side of the centre breast bone and use this centre breast bone to guide the knife in cutting through to the wing joint.

7. The wing is now readily removed from the breast bone and the carcase by pulling and cutting towards the vent or "parson's nose" end.

8. Gently flatten the suprême with a cutlet bat moistened in cold water and knife-trim the edges as necessary.

9. Lightly dredge in sifted, seasoned flour.

10. Heat a tablespoonful of oil in a sauté pan, add the butter and gently fry the suprême without colouring.

11. When the meat is sealed on both sides, add the mushrooms and continue to cook.

12. After 3 or 4 minutes of cooking without colouring, transfer the chicken and mushrooms to a glass fireproof dish (the base of the cloche).

13. Strain away excess oil and butter. Swill the pan with sherry and cream, pour the resultant liquor over the chicken and mushrooms and cover with the cloche.

14. Finish the cooking in the oven. Normally by 5–10 minutes in a hot oven (450° F.).

15. Send the whole glass dish and cloche to table on a d'oyley or napkin-covered silver flat.

For service in the room:

Transfer the glass dish complete with cloche to a warmed meat plate at the guéridon. Then place before the guest and remove the cloche cover at that same moment to the silver flat which is held near the dish. Thus any hot drops of moisture from condensation in the cloche top are caught on the silver dish.

Accompaniments: As this is a pale dish, it is desirable to give it more dramatic impact by adding a slice or two of truffle or a "turned" mushroom before the cloche is put into position. Certainly the dish calls for colourful vegetable accompaniments such as pimento, bright greens, glazed carrots and so on.

Note: Cooking times may vary according to the chef's technique
    for some like to ensure that most cooking is accomplished
    on the stove top with a relatively short time in the oven.
    Some chefs also sweat either chopped onion or shallot to-
    gether with the mushrooms whilst others omit the flour-
    ing of the suprêmes preferring to sauter them "nature". In
    busy kitchens there is also a tendency to use chicken velouté
    in addition to cream. It is also apparent that sherry may be
    varied by using brandy or other liquors to impart flavour.

FAISAN À LA CRÈME SOUS CLOCHE

Perhaps somewhat less hackneyed than chicken for cloche treatment, pheasant being prone to dryness is also eminently suitable
for it. The preparation of the pheasant breasts as suprêmes and the
subsequent treatment is fundamentally the same as for *Suprême de
volaille sous cloche*.

A variation is to lay the pheasant or chicken suprêmes on a
grilled or sauté gammon rasher cut to similar size before completion under the glass.

Pheasants' and chickens' suprêmes cooked in Smitane style are
commonly completed sous cloche.

CHAMPIGNONS SOUS CLOCHE

Mushrooms (including cèpes and other fungi) may be prepared à
la crème and sous cloche for service as a preliminary luncheon
course, accompanied possibly by rice or nouilles. Alternatively
mushrooms in this style might terminate a meal as a delicate
savoury.

BROCHETTES, KEBAB AND SHASLIK
Shish Kebab

Kebabs are oriental dishes which have their counterpart in the
brochette or skewered dishes of the west. Associated with Turkey
and other countries of the Levant, they are also found much farther
east in India. In Malaysia, Satay is a close relation.

In western restaurants featuring Kebab the designation normally
accorded is Shish Kebab. This Turkish or middle eastern styling
simply describes the mode of cooking for kebab implies grilling
and shish, a skewer.

Clearly there is little limit to the ingenuity by which varieties

of meats, vegetables, fruits and fungus can be assembled on the
skewer for grilling. There is also no limit to the variations which
may be given to an accompanying sauce or to the spicing of
marinades in which meats are previously treated. The barbecue
and barbecue sauce of the New World has kinship with, and
can be brought to bear on, this type of cookery.

Even fish, particularly çollops of lobster or whole scallops,
mussels and cubes of white fish blended with peppers and tomatoes on the skewer can be given brochette or shish kebab
treatment.

Most commonly featured, however, are cubes of lamb or mutton, favoured meat of the middle east, followed closely by
lambs' kidneys, pieces of lambs' liver, chicken liver. Used for
further garnish and flavour are pieces of aubergine (egg plant),
green and red peppers, dates, bay leaf, thyme, tomatoes and
mushrooms. Western additions may include sliced, pickled walnuts, chestnuts, stoned prunes, chunks of pineapple, and these
indicate the possibilities of further variation. Koefte or kofta
kebab (spelling varies in differing countries of the east), feature
tiny croquettes of pounded and spiced meat, usually lamb. Kebabs are not normally flambé-d but there is, of course, no reason
why skewered foods may not be so treated on presentation.

Kebab skewers are usually from 6 to 8 ins. long; those of lesser
size are rather unpractical. Skewers for service in the restaurant
are now available elaborated from the simple French type brochette. They are available with decorative handles such as those
resembling tiny swords and so on. Hatelets, those skewers with
elaborately designed handles normally used for buffet presentation are in miniature forms also sometimes used nowadays for
kebab and brochette work.

A basic shish kebab adapted for use in a western restaurant is
likely to feature lamb cubes from the leg (trimmed of fat, bone
and gristle) and marinated for a few hours in a spicy marinade.
The meat, alternating on the skewer with sliced onion, peppers,
mushroom and tomato is served on riz pilaff.

A Montreal restaurant, Aux Quatre Coins du Monde, which
features dishes of the middle east, lists on its menu a fish kebab,
Balut Kebab, consisting of skewered scollops basted in wine sauce.
This restaurant describes its *Shish kebab flambé* as "Le clou de la
soirée".

In serving kebabs and skewered foods generally observe the guidance given in the mode of preparation and service of the following brochette dish:

BROCHETTES DE ROGNONS FLAMBÉES À L'ARMAGNAC

Veal or lambs' kidneys	Bacon
Chicken livers	Salt, pepper
Butter or oil	Thyme, bay leaf
Mushrooms	

In the kitchen:

1. Prepare the sheep's or veal kidneys by clearing away fat, gristle and membrane. Similarly trim the chicken livers.

2. Cut the kidneys to the size of the chicken livers and the bacon (or ham) to cubes of similar width.

3. Select mushrooms of equal diameter and also of similar width and remove stalk. (One mushroom may be "turned" to top the skewer decoratively.)

4. Butter or oil the skewer and fix on alternate seasoned pieces of mushroom (start with the "turned" one), kidney, bay leaf, bacon, thyme, chicken liver.

5. Brush with melted butter or oil and grill—preferably over charcoal.

6. Rest the skewer ends on the grill bars (rather than the meats and garnish) to avoid sticking.

In the room:

1. Pour over each skewer a warmed dessertspoonful of armagnac and ignite.

2. To serve: Hold skewer handle with napkin, and lay the skewer almost flat on the diner's plate, slide fork behind the top mushroom to hold the skewered ingredients firmly. Withdraw the skewer firmly and steadily by pulling on the handle. Do *not* attempt to push off the ingredients.

Accompaniments: Riz pilaff

Normally rice is the accompaniment and is placed first on the plate and prior to this operation.

Shaslik

Fundamentally shaslik differs not at all from shish kebab and is simply the skewering of meat on a sword for subsequent broiling and, these days, normally flambé-ing. The same types of alternating meats and garnishes used for kebabs on skewers can be used for shaslik work though, naturally, because of the longer length of the sword skewer, more than one portion can be prepared at once. It is, moreover, quite commonplace for the meats and garnishes to be cut in somewhat larger cubes so as not to seem disproportionate to the sword size. A note about shaslik swords is included in the earlier chapter on Equipment and Staff. Readily available in many countries of the world including U.S.A. and Germany it may be necessary to have shaslik swords made to order in Britain. As the shaslik tradition is associated with Eastern Europe and Russia, shaslik is often designated *Shaslik Caucasien* or *Shaslik à la russe* on menus.

OTHER PRESENTATIONS

En papillotte

The chief skills in dishes cooked en papillotte are clearly evidenced behind the scenes in the kitchen. This method can be applied to chicken suprêmes and small cutlets of veal or lamb and to escalopes but such meat items require pre-cooking. Paper-envelope treatment is, therefore, especially suitable for work with fish, commonly trout or red mullet, which can be placed raw into its casing. A classic dish of this order is *Rouget en papillotte* (red mullet in paper casing).

The mode of cooking is basically simple though tricky to achieve successfully. The well oiled or buttered fish or meat (par-cooked) is seasoned and wrapped in a shaped paper, normally circular, so that it may fold to a semi circular size and the paper edges crimped and folded in chausson (or pasty) style.

A dish en papillotte must be presented at the table still in its paper casing. Thus it can be pierced and opened by the waiter by running the sharp point of a knife just above the crimping. This enables the top to open as a lid and releases the appetising cooking vapour for the full benefit of the guest.

OMELETTES AND SOUFFLÉS EN SURPRISE

The nearest thing today to the medieval banqueting delight of a dwarf leaping from a pie is, perhaps, the omelette or *Soufflé surprise*, though, perhaps, this hot/cold sweet has degenerated into something of a banquet cliché. Usually the designation omelette is given when the dish and confection is oval in shape and the title *Soufflé surprise* for precisely the same preparation when it is round.

Insulated against oven heat by a base of genoise sponge and an outer casing of meringue, ice cream survives the fire to produce a wide range of dishes fundamentally the same but accorded designations such as *Omelettes* or *Soufflés en surprise milord, milady* or *Norvégienne*. Of the same ilk are Baked Alaska, *Boule de neige* and a score of others.

Most spectacular are those omelettes *en surprise* which have the further spectacle of a flaming fruit top. Of this kind *Soufflé grand succès, Soufflé volcano, Soufflé jubilee* and *Soufflé belle nuit* are, perhaps, better known and differ from each other in only minor degrees.

SOUFFLÉ VOLCANO

The combination of ice-cold interior, hot exterior and a top in flames has dramatic impact. *Soufflé volcano*, basically a simple concept is made as follows.

In the kitchen:

> On the centre spot of an oval dish, place a 4-in.-high pedestal of bread shaped to the diameter of a small silver timbale and cupped at the top to allow the timbale to fit securely. Around this pedestal arrange a bed of genoise sponge to cover the remaining part of the dish and of a depth approximately 2 ins. high. With the timbale in position but empty, arrange around the pedestal alternating portions of vanilla and strawberry ice cream to achieve a mountainous effect. Pipe over an Italian meringue so as to cover the whole of the ice cream to mask the pedestal but to leave exposed the recess for the timbale. Achieve decorative effect with the star tube, sprinkle with icing sugar and bake in a sharp oven to golden brown. Fill the timbale with a blend of hot, stoned cherries and warm Melba sauce.

In the room:

On entering the restaurant or immediately prior to presentation at table, add a measure of Kirsch from a warmed sauceboat and flame. Serve from the guéridon.

FONDUE

FONDUE NEUCHÂTELOISE

Ingredients per person:

¼ lb. Emmenthal or Gruyère cheese (or mixture of both)
1 liqueur glass kirsch
Pepper
Clove garlic

1 hock glass Neuchâtel white wine (vin d'Alsace is suitable substitute)
Little fécule (about a ½ teasp.)

Method:

1. Rub an earthenware fondue pot with garlic.
2. On the fondue stand begin to heat the white wine.
3. Over low flame, add the grated cheese as the white wine heats.
4. Mix the fécule to a smooth flowing paste with the kirsch.
5. When the cheese is melted and bubbling add the fécule and kirsch mix, continuing to stir constantly.
6. After a moment or two's simmering and stirring, the fondue is ready.

Variants: Further flavourings include a little mustard or meat glaze. Some versions, though not true fondues, include egg yolks stirred in with the cheese and added butter. Several slightly differing versions of fondue (minor changes in spicing and garnish) are given local or regional names.

Accompaniments:

Cubes of bread or small chunks from a ficelle loaf, toast or butter-fried croûtons and kirsch for drinking. Diners spear the bread cubes (or other dunking garnish) on a long fork and dip in the pot.

Footnote: Many variants of fondue are prepared in France particularly in the region that borders Switzerland. In his *Phy-
siologie du Goût*, Brillat-Savarin expatiates on fondue and
gives a method of preparing it. A *Fondue de Belley* (Savarin's
birthplace though not his recipe) has also been recorded. It
is a version elaborated with whites and yolks of egg separately whisked and combined not only with grated Gruyère
but with roast fowl gravy and with the truffles of the
area of the Bugey. All this is well whisked together during
cooking and enriched by the addition of butter (monté au
beurre).

FONDUE BOURGUIGNONNE

Authentic methods of preparing fondue Bourguignonne, which
allegedly derives from the old-time quick snacks of Burgundian
peasants, are not easily acquired or verified. It is, in any case,
doubtful whether this meat fondue is altogether suitable for
guéridon work.

Basically, the operation hinges on a bubbling mix of butter and
oil in which cubes of seasoned, beef fillet (about ¾–1 in.) may be
dipped for sauté-ing to the eater's choice. Chopped shallot or
onion and chopped parsley may also be blended with this sauté.
Finally the cooked meat cubes are speared with a long fork by
the diner and dipped into a sauce.

These days a medley of sauces are, especially in U.S.A., provided. Presumably a suitable hot sauce would be a Bourguignonne made with sweated shallots, herbs (parsley, thyme and bay
leaf) and mushroom pieces, red wine reduction, passed and thickened with beurre manié, enriched with further butter and spiced
with cayenne. Nowadays, however, barbecue sauce, blends of
ketchup, derivatives of mayonnaise and a range of bowls con-
taining sauce are often provided. It is anyone's guess as to which
juncture of the meal fondue Bourguignonne may most suitably
be served.

CHEESE AND CHEESE DISHES

For a cheese fondue variant in the British tradition this intrigu-
ingly named dish may be adapted:

ENGLISH MONKEY

1 gill milk	1½ oz. butter
1 egg	¼ lb. grated cheddar cheese
¼ lb. white breadcrumbs	Salt, pepper, nutmeg

In the room:

1. Have a ravier ready with breadcrumbs soaked in milk and a glass goblet for the beaten egg.
2. Using a fondue stand and pot, melt the butter over a moderate flame.
3. Add cheese, stirring as it melts, together with milk soaked breadcrumbs and seasoning.
4. When thoroughly hot and melted finish with lightly beaten egg (without allowing to boil) and adjust the seasoning.

Serve with butter-fried sippets or finger toast.

WELSH RABBIT OR RAREBIT

This old style British cheese dish is perhaps tastier when finished under the salamander but may be prepared on a fondue stand.

Ingredients:

Butter	English mustard
Cheddar cheese	Beer

In the room:

1. Melt butter and over a moderate flame add grated cheese and beer, stirring all the time.
2. Continuing to stir to avoid burning, add prepared English mustard and heat until bubbling. (As cheese itself is salted only a little further salt, if any, should be necessary.)
3. Serve immediately on buttered toast.

Variants: Additional and alternative flavourings include Worcestershire sauce, paprika, nutmeg. If desired a beaten egg may be stirred in just prior to service and the mixture thoroughly restored to heat but without allowing the egg to become cooked hard. Further seasoning will be required if egg is added.

Cheese and Cream Cheese Service

The cheese board, particularly in British restaurants, offers opportunity for attractive presentation though only one of our own varieties, Stilton, really involves a special form of service.

In recent years, indeed, the mode of serving Stilton, napkin wrapped, with top removed, and so that cheese may be scooped from the centre with a special silver scoop has fallen into some disfavour. Reasons against this service are that if the cheese is not consumed reasonably quickly some degree of drying out is inevitable whatever care is given after service.

Another special touch is moistening the interior of Stilton with port. Here again many assert that originally this was merely a device by cunning butlers and maîtres d'hôtel to freshen up a drying cheese. Maybe it is another example of how guests and diners like to be fooled; for there seems to be a greater affection for the resultant pinky-green sludge than is merited. Fine Stilton in good condition marries wonderfully well with a glass of port but, perhaps, the wedding is happier if they are kept apart.

Cream cheese may give some opportunity for exploiting side-table service particularly in the British tradition. The petit suisse of the Continent, dressed in caster sugar and served with fresh cream, is a process simple enough for the guest to do for himself, but perhaps if there was more elaboration of this idea using local cream cheese and with, perhaps, some slight deviations, greater use of this excellent dairy product from our own farms might be promoted. North of Scotland's cream cheese speciality, Crowdie, for example, lends itself to this sort of exploitation. Whilst petit suisse mates well with a little Bar-le-duc jam so some of our own finer conserves can be spooned into a little well in a mound of cream cheese and masked with fresh cream.

Dressings and seasonings also possible as a substitute for cream and conserves include spices such as cinnamon, nutmeg, ginger (including sliced, preserved ginger) and grated chocolate.

CHAPTER 9

SALADS AND THEIR DRESSINGS "IN THE ROOM"

Salads are important items in catering and especially are they so in the present era when they conform perfectly with modern concepts of dining. The trend to simplicity and lightness given impetus and direction in the early part of this century by Escoffier, has tended to increase the use of salads not only as an accompaniment to roasts or as an adjunct to cold dishes but as an alternative or an addition to vegetables at luncheons, dinners and suppers.

Types of Salad

Such is the range and extent of salad preparation that this type of dish may, perhaps, be most conveniently considered divided into the following categories:

1. *Salades simples:* These simple or plain salads are normally composed of greenstuffs or salad vegetables alone and are usually of one or at most two ingredients. Different types of lettuce are typical of components of plain, green salad but there is, of course, a wide range of simple or single salads dressed in various styles featuring tomato, potato and other root and leaf vegetables (particularly shredded cabbage for *Cole Slaw*).

2. *Salades composées.* These blended or compound salads combine a variety of ingredients often featuring shell fish, fish, chicken and meat, fungi, cheese or fruits, and are invariably blended with an appropriate dressing, often a mayonnaise or a derivative of mayonnaise.

3. *Salades de fruits:* Whilst fruit is often an ingredient of a
compound salad the fruit salad used as a sweet item as distinct from an accompaniment of a main or savoury dish is
also an important feature of modern catering.

It will be appreciated that the three different types of salad constitute a substantial section of kitchen and catering work and it is,
therefore, as well to establish immediately that this chapter is
concerned only with those aspects of salad preparation and service
that may commonly impinge substantially upon the work of
waiting staff and which may be regarded as appropriate for guéridon or visual preparation and service in the room.

To all intents and purposes, therefore, the range of compound
salads may be left to the chef and his staff; though there may be a
case for a certain degree of "assembly" of the ingredients for, say,
a lobster salad or chicken salad in the restaurant. Similarly, the
work of peeling and preparing fruit for fruit salads is generally
best left to the pâtissier and his staff though, here again, final
touches such as the addition of kirsch are obviously suitable for the
chef de rang waiter or the station head waiter to perform before
the guest. Thus it is the salades simples with which the restaurateur is chiefly concerned within the room itself.

Whilst bearing in mind the foregoing points it may, further, be
asserted that the most important salad work from the guéridon
or in the restaurant itself consists normally in the preparation of
the dressing (or the blending or finishing of dressings) and subsequently in incorporating or blending those dressings with the
salad ingredients.

Gastronomic and Promotional Aspects

Much of the guéridon work already discussed in preceding
chapters may have been prompted as much by merchandising
aspects as by gastronomic logic. That is to say, that many of the
features of flambé dishes, lamp cookery and of carving may be
strongly motivated by the desire to promote the impact and sale
of dishes by dramatic means. In many instances, eye appeal is
probably a factor greater than the discrimination of the palate.

In the case of salad preparation there are, however, purely gastronomic considerations which strongly support final preparations
at the table or at the sideboard. In the case of green salads, for example, there is little doubt that 10 or 15 minutes is the maximum

time which should elapse between blending with the dressing and the actual consumption of the salad. Gourmets differ about the optimum period during which lettuce should macerate in, say, a vinaigrette dressing and opinions range from service immediately after tossing to allowing the tossed salad to stand for from 5–10 minutes.

It is, of course, perfectly possible for these considerations to be met by dressing a salad "behind the scenes" and many caterers know how effectively simple green salads can be given a French dressing by having a bottle of ready-mixed vinaigrette with a pierced cork or stopper by the salad servery. This enables the waiting staff to shake over the dressing as the salad is collected for service and give the salad a final mixing just before service to the customer. Efficient though such a service device may be for large scale operations, it clearly lacks the confidence building aspect important in any establishment with gastronomic pretensions. Moreover, it largely eliminates the possibility of pleasant promotional touches.

Salad Wagon

Another alternative for salad service is the salad wagon or voiture bearing a variety of pre-prepared dressings and also salad greenery and ingredients themselves in bowls chilled over ice containers, This latter device, compromising between "bespoke" dressing making and "behind the scenes" dressing of a large table d'hôte service, may, indeed, become increasingly necessary as a means of giving the effect of maximum personal attention with minimum of trained staff. If a salad wagon is used, the dressing for which methods are given in this chapter may, of course, be employed, but there is little doubt that it will be far more convenient for those preparations to be made in the garde manger or larder section rather than by the waiting staff.

Dressing Salad at Table

There is a story, possibly apochryphal, of a refugee aristocrat from the French Revolution who earned a good living by visiting the houses of the nobility in Britain to prepare and mix salads in the dining room. One food pundit of Victorian times, Sir Henry Thompson, roundly averred that salad making and dressing should be entrusted to no one but the host or hostess and certainly

not to any cook or member of the service staff. Such historic attitudes underlining the need for salads to be carefully blended and
freshly prepared continue to support the case for this work being
executed before the diner at his table. Gourmets, if no others,
continue to demand that in better restaurants some of the salad
work at least will continue to be done in individual style and at the
table itself for some long years to come.

Whilst a recipe for mayonnaise, which ordinarily for convenience would be made in the kitchen, is included in this chapter the
point is stressed that the general notes here are not tended to deal
with the considerable range of preparatory work in the kitchen
necessary to cover the whole of salad making. It is not thought to
be within the scope of this manual to consider, for example, the
preliminary cleaning and treatment of leaves and roots nor the
various cuts and preliminary cooking, let alone to dwell upon the
vital importance of good purchasing and the freshness and crisp-
ness of salad items. It is, however, obvious that restaurateurs and
their staffs should have a good eye for quality, cleanliness and
freshness so that their work is not dissipated on inferior materials.

INGREDIENTS FOR DRESSINGS

Assuming that good quality ingredients in fresh and clean conditions are used for salads it will be apparent that all else largely
depends upon the quality of the dressing. The operative word is,
indeed, quality, for as most dressings are not cooked the flavours
and textures must be of the best. On no account should cheap,
inferior condiments, oils and vinegars be used to dress salads.

Oils

The classic oil in salad dressing is olive oil of the first pressing
and it is possible that it will never yield its place of first choice for
many gastronomes. Yet there are some for whom even the finest
olive oil has a faint taste which lacks appeal. This probably ex-
plains the present day readiness to use good quality alternative
oils particularly corn oil which is light and fresh tasting and even
huile d'arachide (ground nut oil) which can also give highly
satisfactory results if a good quality is chosen. Whatever oil is used
careful attention must be paid to what the eyes and nose can tell
the user about it. The oil should be clean and clear, indeed

sparkling, and should certainly have no strong smell such as is only too often detected when it is inferior and unfresh.

Vinegar and Lemon

The piquancy in a salad dressing is normally achieved by the use, the sparing use, of vinegar, but it is well worth noting what excellent results may come from the use of lemon (or even lime) juice when available.

Malt vinegar is not recommended for salad use but if this should be unavoidable then certainly a natural vinegar, matured in wood and preferably not coloured with caramel, is to be preferred. The choice should, however, always be for a wine vinegar. There is, moreover, no reason why the wine vinegar should not be pre-prepared for the mise en place by flavourings such as tarragon and garlic.

For novelty value in dressings in Britain there is a case for cider vinegar in a speciality dressing.

Mustard

A common ingredient in a wide range of dressings, the term mustard covers such a wide variety of blends that it is important to consider with care the type chosen for a particular preparation. For dressings designed to have a sharp bite even a simple mixed English mustard is perfectly appropriate. For a blander mix, then a moutarde douce, the darker coloured, and softer flavoured French mustard, will be the choice. Here again there are many varieties and not all of the "reproduction" douce French mustards manufactured outside France manage to achieve a successful flavour.

By far the most generally useful mustard particularly for vinaigrette style dressings is a moutarde forte de Dijon. This is a yellow mustard strong by French standards but by no means so sharp as the English one. If used with discretion it normally gives the right degree of "bite" to a vinaigrette. Whilst there may be a "gimmick" value in using some of the less common French mustards such as green mustards and the tomato flavoured ones, it is seldom that they can add greatly, if at all, to the quality of a dressing to achieve consistent results. It is, therefore, recommended that the choice is confined to French manufactured mustard, preferably Dijon forte, but also blander types, achieving strength of taste by adjustment of quantity used.

Herbs and Seasonings

Much can be done to vary the appeal of a salad by the addition of herbs and seasonings either mixed within the dressing or added to the salad when it is dressed. The use of some of the rarer herbs may perforce have to be left to the domestic cook or hostess in private houses for it is not quite so easy to ensure the availability and fresh preparation of some of the more recherché items for regular restaurant use. Chopped chives, spring onions, fennel, tarragon and even chopped mint are, however, examples of common herbs which may be given a place in the restaurateur's mise en place. Horseradish, olives, grated cheese, ketchups, chutneys, tobasco, chili sauce, soy and Worcestershire sauces, are elements which have been introduced into salad dressings.

As for basic seasoning, whilst the availability of good quality free running salt offers no difficulty, the pepper used is a matter for some consideration. Indeed, the use of pepper in preparing and dressing a green salad is one of the small factors suggesting the desirability of guéridon practice, because when peppercorns are used through the mill they remain as visual specks on a salad. These specks are, of course, completely acceptable when their source has been clearly seen. Certainly, a selection of peppers, including white and black peppercorns in separate mills, and cayenne and paprika also available, is important for salad preparation. In the case of reaction against the coarse graining of pepper from the moulin, pots of ground white as well as pots of ground black or grey pepper should also be available.

Ingredients for Décor

Elaborate garnish of simple salads is not required but decorative use may be made of simple ingredients such as chopped herbs (chives, mint, parsley, tarragon) and contrasting greenstuffs. A simple topping on each plate of half a lemon sliver, asparagus tips, cucumber slices, quartered pineapple slice or the like, with the edge dipped in paprika, parsley or momosa egg can be effective.

Chapon

The term chapon describes the small piece of bread, preferably a neat cube or roundel from a crust which is well rubbed with garlic. Its use is to impart into a salad a flavour of garlic that is not overpowering. The chapon is put in the bottom of a salad bowl so that it mingles with the greenstuffs during the tossing or mixing. In restaurant service, the chapon is not served on to the individual salad plates.

The chapon, pre-prepared in the kitchen, is not, perhaps, as widely used at the guéridon as it might be and certainly it is an appropriate way of imparting a delicious suspicion of garlic during room mixing. Otherwise garlic is neither an easy nor indeed a suitable item for preparing or using at the side table. Rubbing the bowl with a crushed clove of garlic is, in fact, an admirable way of imparting this flavour but is, perhaps, less simple to achieve in guéridon service than "behind the scenes".

General Points in Dressing-making

Perhaps it should be made clear at the outset that a simple, basic oil and vinegar French dressing, a vinaigrette, is widely appreciated by most discerning guests and is generally preferred without fussy elaborations. Restaurateurs must, therefore, incorporate variations with some thought and with some caution. They will certainly be naïve to believe that a multiplicity of additions will necessarily effect an improvement. The same is true of extensions to or adaptations of mayonnaise and its classic derivatives. Despite this emphasis on basic simplicity there is no doubt that the little extra touch, and even a little extra time given to blending a dressing and designed to give a flavour more sophisticated than that which the guest may be bothered to achieve in his or her own home, is likely to repay the effort made.

In blending dressings in the room there is scope for individuality and there is certainly no reason why maîtres d'hôtel and their staffs should not experiment, adapt and blend, using their imagination and flair.

Nowadays, dressings are usually blended together before adding to the salad but when ingredients are added separately the rule is always: oil first until all leaves glisten softly with a film of oil, followed by vinegar (sparingly) and seasoning. The golden rules should be, however, to achieve success through simple blending and to attempt either to meet individual needs of known guests or to work to consistent formulae. Much of the impact is in the visual preparation rather than in complicating the components. Small amounts for individual portions may even be successfully mixed in the bowl of a large service spoon. No restaurateur, therefore, need apologise for confining himself to the proven and basic dressings rather than devising his own.

TYPES OF DRESSING

Restaurateurs and guests alike have their idiosyncrasies and one must allow for these. There are undoubtedly many guests for whom a slightly sweet or sweet dressing is most acceptable. Nevertheless, as a general rule it should be regarded as undesirable to add sugar to a basic vinaigrette; for this alters and virtually destroys the real characteristic of that standard dressing. Certainly, the guest should be asked whether he wishes a sweetened vinaigrette, for it is all too often added in misconceived and excessive zeal.

Salad dressings might, perhaps, be divided into the following groups:

1. *Vinaigrette* (sometimes called French dressing) and its derivatives and deviations.

2. *Thinned mayonnaise* with or without additional flavourings and garnishes.

3. *Sour or acidulated cream* based dressings.

4. *Cheese dressings* (including cream cheese) and blended with ketchups and so on.

5. *Hard boiled egg dressing.*

6. *Cooked dressings.* Kitchen prepared, cooked dressings are usually little more than roux, flour or cornflour thickened white sauces with varying additions which will certainly include vinegar, mustard and seasonings and possibly added oil and egg yolk. They have little application to high class restaurant work.

7. *Sweet dressings.* These are rarely more than amalgams of the other types of dressing to which sugar has been added. Sweetened dressings are not favoured by gourmets.

Cooked dressing, as noted above, has little place in guéridon service except in so far as some speciality of this kind might be provided from a dressing trolly or wagon. Sweet dressings also are not recommended. There can, however, be little doubt that public demand, affected perhaps by American taste for an extension of dressings to accompany the salads which are so popular in the New World, must influence the restaurateur. Modern restaurateurs are increasingly inclined, therefore, to include some of these dressings as appreciated by the American palate in their repertoire.

The purpose of this section is not in any case to pass culinary judgments but rather to indicate basics for salad preparation capable of being extended and varied according to the imagination and ingenuity of restaurateurs and maîtres d'hôtel. Some examples of types long used in U.S.A. and possibly less frequently exploited in Britain are included here as a basis for further experiment and adaptation.

By far the most suitable, useful and important for dressing plain salads in the classic tradition in the room is the vinaigrette and its derivatives, closely followed by the mayonnaise and its group, which also has important application in guéridon work for the seafood cocktails which were separately considered earlier in the book. Vinaigrette, desirably at its simplest and with minimum vinegar, should be the dressing used for salads designed for eating with hot roasts and steaks.

VINAIGRETTE—BASIC DRESSING

3 tablesp. salad oil	$\frac{1}{2}$ teasp. strong Dijon mustard
1 dessertsp. wine vinegar	A dash ground pepper
$\frac{1}{4}$ teasp. salt	

Method: Blend together mustard, salt, pepper and vinegar. When the salt dissolves, add the salad oil, gradually whisking to incorporate it as an emulsion.

For a simple vinaigrette this is commonly garnished with a sprinkling of finely chopped herbs.

Variants for Vinaigrette

Amongst the ingredients which can be added in small quantities to vinaigrette are the following:

Chopped green or red peppers	Capers
Finely diced celery	Finely chopped hard boiled
Grated horseradish	egg
Chopped gherkin	Shredded or chopped carrot
Chopped parsley, chopped tarragon and other herbs.	Finely minced onion, shallot or chives

The following are examples of variants on the basic vinaigrette dressing:

VINAIGRETTE JARDINIÈRE: add a mix of chopped vegetables as a light garnish.

RAVIGOTE DRESSING: (normally for meats including, for example, calf's head) add finely chopped shallots, parsley, chervil, tarragon, chives and capers.

REMOULADE DRESSING: add chopped anchovy fillets, parsley and capers and a suspicion of finely chopped crushed garlic.

NIÇOISE DRESSING: add chopped anchovy fillet, finely diced olives, capers and a touch of crushed, chopped garlic.

CAESAR DRESSING

This dressing of vinaigrette style is especially popular in America for use with Caesar salads, i.e. plain green salads, cos lettuce or romaine. Versions vary but fundamentally it involves incorporating two or three chopped anchovy fillets into the basic vinaigrette above, with a suspicion of garlic and a touch of horseradish cream. Some substitute English mustard for Dijon. A final touch is to break a one-minute boiled egg over, but the dressing is good without this. The Caesar dressed salad may be completed by sprinkling with the moulin, with grated parmesan and with lemon juice.

MAYONNAISE—BASIC RECIPE

Ingredients for 1 pint:

2 large egg yolks	Pinch finely ground pepper
1 tablesp. vinegar	1 pint salad oil
½ teasp. English mustard	Dash lemon juice
¼ teasp. salt	

Method:

1. Have all the ingredients at the same room temperature.
2. Place the egg yolks in a salad bowl and mix with half the vinegar and all the mustard and salt.
3. Whisking briskly, add the oil gradually but steadily in a thin stream. Alternate with a little vinegar if it becomes too thick.

4. When thoroughly mixed and emulsified mix in the remaining vinegar and lemon juice gradually and adjust the piquancy and seasoning to taste.

This basic mayonnaise sauce is almost of whipped cream consistency and for salad dressing must be thinned with cream (or milk) to flowing consistency and the seasoning again adjusted.

Blended and Garnished Dressings with Mayonnaise

Using mayonnaise as a base, flavourings and additives may be added by the restaurateur to make individualistic dressings which may have customer appeal. It has to be faced that these dressings, as in the case of seafood cocktail sauce (from which they are almost indistinguishable except in the point of consistency) tend to rely on bottled ketchups, manufactured sauces and patent flavourings.

An example of a type of blend which may serve to indicate further possibilities is as follows:

To $\frac{3}{4}$ pint mayonnaise add:

  a pinch of salt, cayenne pepper
  1 tablesp. tomato ketchup (approx.)
  Dash of lemon juice, Tobasco and Worcestershire sauce

THOUSAND ISLAND DRESSING (MAYONNAISE BASED)

The precise formula for this dressing is difficult to isolate as so many versions exist. It is basically mayonnaise thinned out and flavoured by chili sauce and, sometimes, ketchup with some additional garnishing. One version is to mix together:

$\frac{1}{2}$ pint mayonnaise
Pinch of the following:

  Minced onion
  Chopped parsley
  Chopped green pepper, olives and/or gherkins
  Chopped hard boiled eggs
  1 teasp. chili sauce

Another version of Thousand Island dressing amalgamates cooked, diced and chopped lobster coral with vinaigrette, shallots, hard boiled egg, parsley and tarragon, but a mayonnaise base is most usual and generally considered authentic.

MAYONNAISE DRESSING À L'INDIENNE

Curry powder or well reduced, strong curry sauce may be introduced into mayonnaise with good effect and further interesting blends may be achieved by using as a substitute or as additional flavours some of the Indian chutneys and pickles now available. Chopped hot mango Kasundi and chopped lime pickle are particularly useful.

CREAM DRESSINGS

SOUR CREAM MAYONNAISE

½ pint mayonnaise	Seasoning
2 tablesp. cream (sour or acidulated)	Teasp. (approx.) chopped chives

This blend is made by mixing together the ingredients, adjusting the seasoning with additional salt and pepper with possible dusting of dressed salad with paprika and other items for colour contrast.

Gloucester sauce, which may be used as a dressing is similarly made, but with chopped fennel in lieu of chives.

SOUR OR ACIDULATED CREAM DRESSING

3 tablesp. cream
Salt, pepper
1 tablesp. lemon juice (or vinegar or lemon and vinegar mixed)
Method:
  Blend together the basic ingredients.

SPANISH CREAM DRESSING

½ pint cream	Salt, pepper
1 teasp. English mustard	1 lemon
1 teasp. caster sugar	

Method:
  Blend together the mustard, sugar and the strained lemon juice

  Stir in the cream gradually
  Season to taste with salt and with pepper if required.

Variants:

Either of the above two simple cream dressings may be regarded as a starting point for individual extensions. Tarragon, chives and even ketchups and bottled sauces and flavourings may be incorporated to taste.

CHEESE DRESSINGS

CREAM CHEESE DRESSING

2 oz. cream cheese
Salt, pepper
½ pint basic vinaigrette

1 teasp. (approx.) grated horse-radish

This basic cream cheese dressing is made by adding the ingredients gradually to the cheese so that a smooth texture is achieved. Horseradish may be varied to increase or decrease the hot tang and it is obvious that it may be omitted, and items such as chopped chives, chopped tarragon and other herbal flavourings substituted. For Scotland, a Crowdie dressing with individual touches can in England be matched by similar variations in cream cheese from areas of the south.

ROQUEFORT DRESSING

¼ lb. Roquefort
½ pint salad oil
Pinch cayenne

2 tablesp. white wine vinegar
Large teasp. Dijon mustard
Salt

Method:

1. Blend the crumbled Roquefort with Dijon mustard, seasoning and vinegar.
2. Add oil gradually and steadily, beating to a smooth consistency.
3. Adjust the seasoning.

Variants:

There are, of course, many blue cheese dressings, many of them emanating from America where this type of salad accompaniment enjoys much popularity. Satisfactory blue cheese dressings may be made quite simply by incorporating ¼ lb. Danish blue cheese into 1 pint mayonnaise, thinned with cream (or even evaporated milk) with seasoning suitably adjusted. For their own blue cheese dressing, British restaurateurs should not hesitate to experiment with Stilton, English mustard, oil and vinegar of similar proportions.

HARD BOILED EGG DRESSINGS

BASIC HARD BOILED EGG DRESSING

1 hard boiled egg
½ teasp. Dijon mustard
Salt, pepper
1 tablesp. wine vinegar
4 tablesp. oil

Method:

1. Thoroughly pound the separated yolk of the hard boiled egg in a salad bowl.
2. Mix to a paste with the mustard, seasoning and vinegar.
3. Whisk in the oil gradually to form a smooth mixture of creamlike consistency.
4. Garnish with hard boiled egg white cut into fine julienne.

GRIBICHE SAUCE

This variant of hard boiled egg dressing may be made by adding to the basic hard boiled egg dressing a dessertspoonful chopped parsley, tarragon and chervil and a dessertspoonful well drained and chopped (cloth squeezed and dried) gherkin and capers.

WYVERN'S DRESSING

Col. Kenney-Herbert who wrote about food under the *nom de guerre* "Wyvern" was most attentive to correct salad composing. He favoured a hard boiled egg dressing as follows:

2 hard boiled egg yolks
2 raw egg yolks
1 teasp. chopped shallot
½ to ¾ pint oil
1 dessertsp. tarragon vinegar
Pinch salt, pepper
1 teasp. Dijon mustard

Method:

Using a wooden spoon, bruise the minced shallot in the salad bowl together with the mustard, seasoning and the hard boiled egg yolks. To this paste, gradually add oil mixing until you have the consistency of thin batter; then whip in the raw yolks. Con-

Salad Mixing

Mixing a salad from the guéridon may be given additional appeal in summer by being effected with the bowl in a container of ice. Here a large fruit salad container is exploited to good effect for that purpose. To give a dramatic touch a dextrous waiter can learn to rotate the salad bowl on its ice bed when blending the dressing. Note the crescent salad plates are "en place" ready for individual service.

Service of brochette or shish kebab: The waiter serves the lady first but note that both diners have already been helped to rice. The waiter holds the skewered meats firmly in position with the fork and steadily withdraws the skewer. He does *not* push off the food with the fork as this displaces the rice and destroys the symmetry of the food. Note the decorative hatelet used as a brochette or skewer.

The Author with Shaslik Sword

This shaslik sword has been made to specification
in Britain; note both the guard at the hilt and the
cup for flambé-ing liquors and to trap juices.
At the top and bottom of the skewered meats
are movable and securable bolts to keep the food
in position when cooking prior to service.

tinue to beat, adding oil until the total bulk is of about ¾ pint of
sauce of thickly coating consistency. Add the vinegar and the
mixture becomes creamy. Sample for tang and add further vinegar and seasoning to taste.

CAMBRIDGE SAUCE

This sauce is compounded of hard boiled egg, anchovy fillets,
capers, blanched chervil, chives, tarragon and parsley mixed with
mayonnaise and also suggests use for dressing purposes if extended with sour cream.

MIXING SALADS

As the more elaborate composite salads are kitchen prepared they
need little attention in the restaurant other than careful
service. The mixing of salads and their subsequent dressing by
waiting staff chiefly centres, therefore, on green or tossed types;
though it is possible that into some of them may be incorporated
cooked green beans or cooked peas and possibly non-green items
such as radishes and even tomatoes. Green salad stuffs (interpreting
the term "green" loosely) includes not only lettuces of the cabbage, cos and romaine type but chicory, endive, watercress,
mustard and cress, green peppers, celery and so on. Even young,
raw spinach may be used.

General Points in Salad Making

Points to bear in mind when mixing salads either from guéridon
or behind the scenes are:

1. Scrupulous cleanliness by thorough, prior washing.
2. Freedom from moisture after washing. Salad stuffs
should be thoroughly shaken to ensure complete dryness.

An extremely common flaw is attempting to use imper-
fectly dried salad greens. Not only is surplus moisture offen-
sive to the eye and palate but, of course, seriously impairs
the dressing by diluting it.

3. That the ingredients are fresh, crisp and cool.
4. That even for "plain" green salads there is much to be
said for seeking contrast of colour and flavour. Introducing
cress or raw spinach into a lettuce salad not only gives
different shading of green but also introduces a more tangy
flavour.

5. Ensure that the mixing bowl is adequate in size for it is important that there is no attempt to overload with salad stuffs. To mix well and thoroughly greenstuffs must be able to lie loosely and to be capable of free movement.

Implements for Salad Service

Traditionally, wood salad bowls are much favoured as are wooden salad forks and spoons for mixing. An important reason for using implements of such a material was that they were thought to cause less bruising to tender greenstuffs. Certainly wood, horn or similar non-metallic salad servers should be selected rather than metal spoon and fork for salad mixing.

When mixing before the guest there is, however, a case for using a glass bowl as an alternative to wood. An effective means of adding a touch of showmanship is to place a salad mixing bowl on a bed of ice within a container bowl so that the salad may be rotated during the mixing process.

Salad wagons to support such guéridon service are increasingly used and here again double containers are to be recommended for any pre-prepared dressings so that they may be kept chilled on ice. Cooled or chilled bowls, dishes and raviers should always be used for salad service.

Affording facilities for guests to blend their own dressings is also a promotional idea suitable in some types of operation.

As has been noted, garlic is awkward to use within the restaurant. Better, therefore, to rely on chapons (see p. 126) but if garlic is required then a small press is suitable.

The type of stoppered shaker used behind the scenes for pre-prepared dressings may also be used in a smarter version from a salad voiture or from the guéridon where speed is an element of importance.

As was stressed in the introductory paragraphs of this chapter side-table preparation and dressing of salads can fulfil a twin purpose. First, to ensure the freshness and excellence of the blend and, second, to promote business by a little "flair" and show. Happily, these twin purposes are completely compatible.

CHAPTER 10

SIDE TABLE COFFEE AND LIQUEUR SERVICES

By the time a restaurant meal has reached the stage when a guest takes coffee, much has already been done to enhance (or damage) the establishment's reputation. Nevertheless, because last impressions are so important it is vital that interest should be sustained throughout this concluding period of the meal.

In some types of restaurant operation there are additional opportunities for promotional touches at coffee service time. These depend not merely on the offering of cigars and liqueurs— conveniently from a wagon or voiture, but also in the featuring of specialities. Irish coffee (given further consideration below) may be regarded not only as a typically successful example of promotion, but one, moreover, which was developed in these islands, It is of a style and kind compatible with the region in which it is highlighted as a tourist attraction.

Coffee itself is commonly served in such variety of forms that a change from one style to another may give a measure of interest, even without further and special service touches. In a handbook such as this dealing with specialist aspects of service it is thought neither necessary nor desirable to detail the whole principles and practices of coffee-making, important though these are; nor to provide detailed instructions for the service of coffee in the various standard forms. It is, nevertheless, pertinent to note that apart from standard servings of well prepared, hot, strong coffee in hotel plate coffee services, or brown, earthenware coffee pot that other modes of presentation have much merit and command a following. *Café filtre*, Cona and Turkish coffee, for example, may be introduced with advantage according to the size and standard of establishment to increase guest interest at a meal's culmination.

Coffee Filtre
Many discriminating coffee drinkers believe that the service of coffee in individual filtres is overrated. Certainly this form of service all too often leads to coffee less hot than is desirable due to sluggish drip through the grains and filter and to the all too frequent failure adequately to warm both the filter container and the coffee cup receiving the liquid.

Individual filtres are usually made to fit over coffee cups of French style and size rather than the demi-tasse shape commonly used in Britain. It is important to use a good, strong "dinner" roasted coffee and to pre-warm both filter container and cup below.

Cona Coffee
Cona machines have long been appreciated by restaurant staff and guests alike as an extremely reliable way of achieving good coffee, freshly made. Whether heat is provided by spirit lamp or electricity, the machines, furthermore, are visually attractive. They can, therefore, fulfil a promotional aspect within the room.

When Cona coffee is to be prepared at the guéridon for individual parties, it is prudent to use pre-heated water from the still room so that quicker boil over the lamp is achieved. Warm apparatus and warmed cups are required.

Turkish Coffee
Over and above such basic presentations of coffee as the still room made beverage or filtre or Cona there are further styles, additions and elaborations which may be regarded as involving guéridon or side table preparation.

Of these Turkish coffee is a form which has over many years and in many establishments been given prominence. Merchandising has often been aided by an appropriately costumed coffee maker using stylish apparatus. Where at one time the Turkish coffee maker was male and eastern, nowadays attractively garbed girls may feature in this special service as is the case, for example, in the Istanbul Hilton.

Basically Turkish coffee is a form of making the beverage in a pot or pan. Any small vessel of this kind may, therefore, be regarded as suitable for it. In restaurant work it is, however, clearly desirable in order properly to promote and feature this form of coffee to have appropriate equipment in authentic middle-eastern style.

A Turkish coffee trolly or guéridon would require brass or copper tray with matching lamp stand, small Turkish, lipped coffee pots of narrowing neck with long handle; vessel for water and receptacles for sugar and coffee. Beaten and chased metal, sometimes with elaborate inlay, are commonly used to give decorative effect.

As western style coffee making techniques vary, so in Turkish coffee making even middle-eastern devotees differ in their modes. Perhaps the following method of a young Turkish hotel man, Mr Basak Oktar, is as generally acceptable as any:

TURKISH COFFEE, SWEETENED

To serve 2 people or to yield 2 small coffee cups, put 2 cups (coffee size) of cold water in the coffee pan and boil the water over the open flame or fire.

When boiled, pour enough water back in the cups to one-third fill them.

Allow 2 teaspoonsful of sugar per person and dissolve in the water still in the pan. Add 2 teaspoonsful of pure ground Turkish coffee per person and stir once or twice. Bring to the boil.

At this stage be very careful not to overboil; thus just before boiling point is reached add the one-third of water still in the cups and boil for the last time.

Then about half fill each coffee cup, allowing equal amounts of froth in the cups.

Heat the remaining coffee in the boiler and finish pouring to complete the coffee service.

TURKISH COFFEE, UNSWEETENED

Use the same method for unswe_tened Turkish coffee, omitting sugar; but in this case, loaf (or lump) sugar should be offered to the customers in a separate dish. In Turkey the customer takes a loaf or two, bites a piece and drinks his unsweetened coffee dissolving the sugar in his mouth.

This method is particularly customary in the eastern part of Turkey.

ALTERNATIVE METHOD FOR TURKISH COFFEE

One heaped teaspoonful of finely ground coffee per demi-tasse of water with sugar to taste. Turkish coffee is generally served sweet but guests should first be consulted. Though about a teaspoonful is normal, some guests will reject sugar even in Turkish coffee. In this method, the mix is stirred, heated almost to boiling point, and as the froth rises it alone is poured into the warm demi-tasse. The coffee pot is returned to the flame for re-boiling twice more. Surface froth is similarly removed each time before final service of all the coffee into the cups.

THIRD METHOD FOR TURKISH COFFEE

A further alternative is to begin to heat the water, then add in the measure of coffee and sugar and bring to the boil without stirring. Immediately the water boils the infusion is encouraged by stirring away from the heat; then returning to re-boil until a good head of froth appears. As before, this process is repeated and the coffee served with each cup topped with froth. Normally, Turkish coffee is individually made but if two or more portions are prepared together serve a little froth in each cup.

Though not unfailingly done, it is agreeable if a glass of iced water is also offered at the same time as the coffee; and this should not inhibit the service of brandy and liqueurs.

CAFÉ CAPPUCCINO

The chocolate flavoured café Cappuccino is, perhaps, like café Viennoise, more a beverage for occasional mid-morning or mid-afternoon drinking in boulevard café rather than for after-dinner service. However, at least one restaurant does feature it as an after-dinner speciality, for the American *Gourmet* magazine recently published a reader's letter of appreciation of such a service following dinner at the Café Bleu near The Hague in Holland. For café Cappuccino served there, mise en place included with a pot of strong, black coffee is a bowl of whipped cream, a bowl of grated sweet chocolate and sugar. The waiter measures two teaspoons of chocolate to each cup half filled with coffee, stirring until melted. After sweetening to taste, the waiter tops with whipped cream, garnishing the surface with further grated chocolate.

CAFÉ BRÛLÉ OR CAFÉ BRÛLOT

This spiced, flambé-d coffee is a definite example of a lamp or chafing dish performance. Spices and flavourings used may be varied according to individual taste but an example of ingredients is:

1 liqueur glass cognac
4 lumps sugar (impregnated as in crêpe Suzette making by rubbing 2 against the orange zest and 2 against lemon)
2 or 3 cloves and a fragment of cinnamon stick and vanilla pod
2 demi-tasses good, black coffee

To make:

1. Heat a tablespoonful of already roasted and roughly crushed coffee beans over gentle flame until the perfume is discernible.
2. Then remove the pan from the heat, add the sugar lumps and spices and stir in the cognac.
3. When the sugar lumps are broken down and dissolving return to the lamp and continue to heat over a moderate flame.
4. When brandy mixture is hot, ignite and then extinguish the flames by stirring in the hot coffee.
5. For serving small numbers, carefully pour so as to leave behind the débris from the lipped pan into warm coffee cups (use of a small strainer and/or filter paper is optional). For larger numbers the coffee may be transferred to heated coffee pot.

CAFÉ DIABLE

There is really little to distinguish café diable from café brûlot except that diable or devilled coffee may be thought to require a little more pungency. Spices may, therefore, be varied with this in view (even a fragment of root ginger has been introduced by some operators). Alternatively a spicier or "peppery" effect may be achieved by using Chartreuse liqueur in lieu of half the quantity of brandy.

DEMI-TASSE FLAMBÉ À L'ARMAGNAC

A simple mode of serving coffee flambé for individuals may be effected at the guéridon as follows:

1. Gently spoon on to the top of the demi-tasse of hot, black coffee a dessertspoonful of armagnac.
2. Put a lump of sugar in a warm tablespoon, add armagnac and ignite.
3. Place the flaming spoon into the coffee, stirring gently until the flame is extinguished.

IRISH COFFEE

To make the generally accepted version:

To a warmed, 8-oz. glass goblet add a measure of Irish whiskey. Sweeten to guests' taste with one or two coffeespoons of caster or brown sugar. With a spoon in the glass goblet pour in hot, strong black coffee to within an inch of the rim. Stir to mix the coffee and whiskey and to dissolve the sugar. Take fresh double cream and pour gently into the glass so that the cream floats on the surface. Do this by pouring the cream over the up-turned bowl of a coffee spoon or by pouring carefully on to the inner rim of the glass. If the cream is first lightly whipped so that air is incorporated it will facilitate floating.

An elaboration of the service of Irish coffee has been successfully exploited in the Playbill Restaurant of New York's Manhattan Hotel where a larger glass is used. In their presentation, a 16 oz. brandy balloon is first given a coating of whipped cream on the inner and upper half. Then the waiter measures in the Irish whiskey, tops with hot coffee and floats on further whipped cream before service to the guest on an underplate. The restaurant's name for this speciality is Shillelagh.

GAELIC COFFEE, DRAMBUIE COFFEE AND SIMILAR FORMS

It is obvious that the concept of Irish coffee can suggest further presentations; as for example, Gaelic or Scotch coffee using Scotch whisky either blended or single malt. There is no reason why it should not be named Highland coffee or given any local or regional nomenclature.

In the George V in Paris, Drambuie coffee was introduced some time ago. It was made by dissolving a half teaspoon of brown sugar in a measure of Drambuie, stirring gently into hot, black coffee, with thick cream allowed to settle on top.

Brontë coffee, featuring the Yorkshire liqueur is also advocated for similar style service and many black coffees, liqueur laced, can agreeably be sipped through a thick cream topping.

Apart from contrasting liqueurs and spirits used for Irish, Gaelic and Drambuie coffee, other liqueurs commonly served in this style are crème de Cacao and Tia Maria, which is itself coffee flavoured.

SERVICE OF BRANDY AND LIQUEURS

In addition to the standard type of cart or voiture for cigar and liqueur service there have been models specially devised for the preparation and service of Cona coffee and liqueurs from a wagon. A movable service, attractively presented, is naturally an effective way of encouraging impulse buying at a meal's end and when guests should (if all preceding service was successful) be in a mood to make an order with their coffee for brandy, liqueurs and cigars.

BRANDY-GLASS WARMING

Much controversy has raged around the service of brandy. Many connoisseurs even consider that the use of 16 oz. brandy balloons (and certainly larger sizes) is largely pretentiousness. There is no doubt, however, that vast numbers of those who appreciate fine brandy do enjoy cradling the balloon so that the warmth of the hand helps generate the bouquet to be savoured by the nose before sipping.

What is universally deplored nowadays is the use of a flame, particularly methylated spirit flame (methylated spirits and brandy are not exactly compatible bouquets) for pre-warming of the glass.

Unfortunately, some of the gadgets devised for brandy balloon warming—even intended to warm glasses with brandy already in—are of attractive appearance. No doubt because of their handsome look they are, and probably will continue to be, used in restaurant service. Even with this promotional appeal, the treatment of brandy in this way must, however, be deplored, and one of the missionary tasks of the sommelier or wine waiter should be to dissuade guests from indulging in this addiction.

Immersing the brandy balloon in hot water is equally deplorable.

Amongst service touches possible for brandy is the tiny barrel mounted on a wagon or liqueur cart and an older generation may recall sherry served in this style in Bellometti's in Soho.

Pousse Cafés, Champarelles and Scaffas

One of the ways in which liqueur sales may be promoted, many of which have undoubted appeal to women guests, is through featuring one or two pousse cafés. The scope for the different colour and flavour combinations in devising these decorative, "layered" drinks is extremely great and house specialities may be devised once one knows the specific gravity or the way in which one liquid will float upon another. Champarelle and Scaffa are largely indistinguishable from pousse cafés and simply afford an opportunity to vary the name.

Tall, slender liqueur glasses should be chosen for this type of drink or even the tall slender sherry glasses of copita style. The capacity of the glass must, of course, be predetermined so that accurate measurement of each layer can be made with precision to fill the glass as desired. Not each layer need be alcoholic. Fruit syrups such as grenadine and cassis are often the base and one type of pousse café even features an egg yolk layer.

POUSSE L'AMOUR

A layer of maraschino, then a separated but unbroken egg yolk, followed by green Chartreuse and topped with cognac. Each layer slid in carefully either using the rim of the glass or pouring over a spoon surface.

JERSEY LILY POUSSE CAFÉ

An extremely simple pousse café, reputedly favoured by the Edwardian theatrical idol, was simply equal parts Chartreuse and cognac.

POUSSE CAFÉ ARC-EN-CIEL

Others may, however, feature as many as 6 layers and one of the most complex pousse cafés has, not unnaturally been designated arc-en-ciel or Rainbow. It is necessary to check old orders of sequence for layering this and other pousse cafés because of changes in the specific gravities of ingredients. An example of an arc-en-ciel or Rainbow pousse café layers the following equal parts:

Crème de cacao	Chartreuse jaune
Crème de violette	Chartreuse verte
Bénédictine	Maraschino
Cognac	

Blazers

Blazers have not been in fashion during recent years, but blazers additional to the two examples below and using a variety of spirits (particularly brandy, whisky and rum) can be concocted as inn specialities.

BRANDY BLAZER

A flamed brandy is included amongst some cocktail lists though it hardly seems to be an appropriate aperitif and appears better suited to be an after dinner comforter. To make it rub a sugar lump against an orange (or lemon) so that it acquires colour and flavour and stir it in a thick mixing glass with a strip of orange zest and lemon zest and a measure of brandy. Ignite, stir and strain into a brandy glass.

BLUE BLAZES

A flaming toddy may not have a place in smarter restaurants but Blue Blazes could well be featured in a country hotel or inn. Make it as follows: Stir a measure of Scotch, a strip of lemon zest and a sugar lump (or spoonful of honey or syrup) in a thick mixing glass (or silver tankard). Have a quarter tumbler of hot water in a similar mixing glass or a Russian tea tumbler. Flame the whisky mix and pour it flaming into the hot water. The effect should be of a stream of fire. Mix by pouring back and forth from vessel to vessel. Serve with twist of lemon zest.

Last Impressions

When guests are mellow and content at the meal's end, good impressions are consolidated. Small additional touches may bring disproportionately great rewards to the restaurateur. The gratuitous offering of petits fours, a small bon-bon dish of after dinner mint chocolate wafers or similar sweetmeats must be considered.

And just as the welcoming approach on arrival is the chief feature of good service, so is the courteous and warm farewell to the departing guest.

A GUÉRIDON GLOSSARY

Naming and Devising Dishes

Throughout this book emphasis has been placed on the fact that guéridon cookery and flambé work affords opportunity for individuality. Methods are of necessity basically simple and production has to be swift. Much depends on flair, skill and showmanship and this can be further aided by the way in which house specialities are presented on the menu. In a number of establishments a flambé feature bearing its French name carries a brief explanatory note or at least mentions the main ingredients and the liqueurs used for flaming.

Many of the ways of preparing minute steaks or escalopes vary only by a hair's breadth from one establishment to the other and many "differences" hinge only upon the cut or shape of the meat or on the type of spirit or liquor employed. Even these variations, however, are by no means insignificant factors and both appetite of the guest and inventiveness of the restaurateur may well be stimulated by further small touches. Even allowing the mind to dwell on varied menu terms for the small meat cuts such as rosettes, médaillons, cœurs, filet mignon, tournedos, mignonette d'agneau and the like.

In application to veal and pork, though we may encounter a rouelle de veau, words other than escalope are perhaps less easy to find. But dishes of Italian inspiration afford a chance for using piccata, scallopine or saltimbocca. When treating the fillet of chicken one may choose between suprêmes or délices de volaille. Whether we elect poulet or poularde for our lamp work is not always of great significance and though France is often praised for its concise and descriptive menu language there seems little to choose (at least from the language point of view) between

147

Poulet de Bresse flambé au cognac and Surrey chicken flamed in whisky—and the latter can be a genuinely good dish.

Cocktail fruits de mer, or seafood cocktails, may have too much anonymity and we are bound to envy the French who can find such terms as *Demoiselles de Cherbourg* to describe the huge, delicately flavoured shrimps. But having arranged shrimp cocktail to resemble a large rose-like flower one might forgivably call it *Crevettes bouquet*.

It matters little whether a pepper steak is called *Steak au poivre* or *Steak poivrade* and there often seems but minor difference between a monkey gland steak and a steak Diane.

The list of commodities (in Chapter 3), particularly the spirits and liqueurs, may be helpful in suggesting dish designations from a simple "flambé aux aromates" or au liqueur or au vieux marc to any number of specially named brands. There are many orange liqueurs, for example, which make it possible to ring the changes on canard flambé au curaçao for we can specify Cointreau or Grand Marnier and even try mandarine.

The many synonyms or near synonyms in the English tongue for flaming or burning can usefully give variety when naming dishes of our own devising. Whether blazed, fired, flashed, flamed, ignited or even seared, scorched or singed may be of little culinary significance but may give menu distinction. Pyrotechnics in the restaurant bring a train of words like conflagration, fire, aflame, fiery, combustion and also some associated words like firefly, firework, fire worshipper, fire eater, and firebrand which can come to the aid of a maître d'hôtel who wants to name a new creation.

Thus terms such as these and their French equivalent are listed below amongst a few terms additionally useful to the guéridon and flambé operator. The list is not meant to comprise a comprehensive glossary but rather to be an aide memoire and one, perhaps, provocative of ideas for dish making and dish naming.

Generally, words fully dealt with in the general text of the book are not included in the list nor are liqueurs and commodities already listed in Chapter 3.

A LIST OF MENU AND GUÉRIDON TERMS

A

Afire, aflame	Possible designations for flambé dishes
à la grecque	In Greek style (hence *Kebab à la grecque*)
à la turque	In Turkish style (hence *Kebab à la turque*)
à la russe	In Russian style (hence *Shaslik à la russe*)
à ma façon	In my style (describes one's own speciality)
à point	just cooked
al dente (It.)	Expression describing the desired degree of cooking for pastas, i.e. still slightly firm. Literally "to the teeth".
Arson	Unlawfully setting on fire (possible humorous menu use for flambé dish)
au poivre	With pepper, peppered
aux aromates	With aromatic herbs or spices.

B

Bécasse	Woodcock
Bécassine	Snipe
Bien cuit	Well cooked
Bigarade	Seville orange, a type of bitter orange (used in the making of curaçao) and hence a name attached to orange-flavoured sauce dishes. *Sauce bigarade* for use with duck is a re-reduction of the roast gravy, then mainly flavoured with orange and butter
Bitok	Medallion of minced raw meat blended with milk-soaked crumbs, onions, etc., usually served *à la russe*, i.e. with creamy Smitane sauce
Blaze, blazes, blazing	English words for possible menu use for flambé dishes.
Blazer	The frying pan or skillet used on the lamp or as part of chafing dish
Bleu	Very underdone (for grills); literally blue
Bolide	Meteor, ball of fire
Brandon	Firebrand
Brûlant	Burning

Brûlé	Burnt
Brûlement	Burning (noun)
Brûlerie	Burning (noun)
Brûleur	An incendiary
Brûloir, brûloire	Burner, roaster
Brûlot	Firebrand
Brûlure	A burn or scald.

C

Canard	Duck
Canard sauvage	Wild duck
Caneton	Duckling
Chaslyk	Alternative spelling of shaslik
Chauffe-assiettes, Chauffe-plats	Plate warmer or dish warmer
Chaufferette	Chafing dish
Cœur	Heart, also used to describe dainty cut of beef fillet, e.g. *Cœur de Charolais*, or cœur de laitue, lettuce heart
Collop	A slice or cut (for example of veal), escalope
Compôte	Stewed fruit
Confiture	Jam
Crevettes bouquet	Big rose shrimps
Crevette (grises)	Shrimps, hence *cocktail de crevettes*
Crevettes roses	Prawns.

D

Déglace	Deglaze
Délice	Delicate portion, i.e. fillet, particularly of fish or chicken
Demi-glace	High quality brown sauce. Literally half glaze (meat)
Demi-tasse	Small coffee cup (literally half cup)
Démon	Demon, fiend
Diable	Devil (hence *café diable*, devilled coffee)
Doux, douce	Sweet, soft, mild, e.g. *moutarde douce*
Duxelle	A mixture of minced mushrooms and shallots cooked in butter, used to stuff tomatoes, etc.

E

Enfer	Hell (*un feu d'enfer*—a scorching, scathing fire)
en feu	On fire
Enflammer	To fire, to flame
en tasse	On cup.

F

Faux feu	Flash in the pan
Feu	Fire
Feu d'artifice	Fire-work
Feu de Bengal	Bengal (blue) light
Feu de joie	Bonfire
Feutier	Fire attendant
Filet mignon	Fillet from the saddle of lamb or mutton. Sometimes used to describe a dainty steak cut from beef fillet
Flambant	Blazing, flaming
Flambé	Flamed, flared
Flambeau	Torch
Flamber	To flame, to blaze, to flare, hence *flambé*, flamed
Flamboiement	Flare, flaming (noun)
Flamboyant	Flaming, blazing
Flamboyer	To flare, to flash, to blaze
Flamme	Flame
Flammèche	Spark
Flammerole	Fire-drake, will-o'-the-wisp
Flammette	Little flame
Fourré	Stuffed (when applied to foods)
Fruits de mer	Literally "fruits of the sea", describes mixed variety of fish, hence cocktail fruits de mer.

G

Garde manger	Larder
Genoise	A type of sponge cake made from sugar, flour, butter and eggs

Glace de viande	Meat glaze
Grenadin	A cut of veal, similar to escalope
Gros sel	Coarse salt, freezing salt
Guèbre	Fire worshipper
Guéridon	Guéridon, in restaurants refers to the service side table; otherwise in general use a guéridon is a round table with single central foot or pedestal. It was also used for the playing of the old card game of loo. According to *Petit Larousse* the name guéridon derives from that of a "personnage" de comédie.

H

Hades	Hell
Holecauste	Burnt offering.

I

Ignicole	Fire worshipper
Ignition	Ignition
Ignivome	Vomiting fire (adj.)
Ignivore	Fire-eating
Incendiaire	Incendiarist.

J

Jus	Gravy or juice
Jus lié	Thickened gravy.

K

Kebab	Skewered grill or charcoal-roast.

L

Lampyre	Fire-fly
Liaison	Thickening or binding
Lié	Thickened (hence *jus lié*, thickened gravy).

M

Maison	House; hence *à la maison*, in the style of the house
Marinade	A pickling or seasoning liquor for steeping (marinating) meats as in kebab preparation. Marinades are usually made from oil, wine, vinegar, herbs and spices
Marron	Chestnut
Médaillons	Round, flat portions of meat
Météore	Fireball, meteor
Mignon	Neat, delicate, tiny (hence *mignon de bœuf*, small neat cut of fillet steak)
Mignonette	Ground pepper (also used as diminutive of mignon)
Montmorency	Denotes presence of cherries in sauce or garnish (associated with duck dishes).

N

Neige	Snow. Poached meringue may be so described, hence *neige flambé*
Noisette	Nut, or when applied to meat cuts, boneless, neat cut from loin or carré.

P

Piccata (It.)	Small escalope, normally of veal
Paprika	Mild, red pepper
Piperade	A pan-made dish of eggs of southern France, especially *piperade basquaise*, "Basque omelette"
Poivrade	Flavoured with pepper, hence steak *poivrade*
Poivre, au	With pepper, hence steak *au poivre*
Point, à	Just cooked
Pojarski	Minced veal re-assembled in cutlet form
Pompier	Fireman
Poularde, poulardine	Young, fat chicken
Poulet	Young chicken
Poussin	Chick, immature chicken

Prosciutto (It.)	Italian smoked ham (the best is from Parma), popularly served with melon (*Prosciutto e melone*) or green figs (*Proscuitto e fichi*)
Pryophage	Fire-eater
Pyrotechnie	Pyrotechny, pryotechnics (art of making, displaying fireworks).

R

Ravier	Literally radish dish, used to describe *hors d'œuvre* dish
Réchaud	Chafing dish
Réchauffer	To heat again, hence *rechauffé*, reheated
Réchauffoir	Dish or plate warmer
Recherché	Out of the ordinary, choice
Rosette (*de bœuf*)	Literally rosette or small rose but used to describe choice, dainty small round cut from fillet of beef or similar delicate portion of meat
Rouelle	A round slice or escalope (normally if meat of veal or pork) i.e. *rouelle de citron*, slice of lemon.

S

Saignant	Underdone
Saltimbocca (It.)	Thin escalopes (from veal fillets) joined or skewered to similar sized thin slices of ham and quickly pan-fried
Scallopine di Vitello (It.)	Escalopes of veal
Scorched, seared, singed	Possible menu words for flamed dishes
Shaslik, shaslyk	Anglicised spellings of this Caucasian dish vary, as do recipes according to the region of the Caucasus. Shaslik are, however, normally metal skewers (though in some parts thin wooden ones are used)
Shish Kebab	Cubed meat skewered and charcoal grilled or roasted

Skillet	Frying pan
Souvlakia	Greek dish of cubed, skewered and grilled meat
Spaghetti alla Veneziana (It.)	Spaghetti in Venice style (i.e. with tomato sauce, Parmesan cheese).

T

Torche	Torch
Torchère	Torch, candelabrum
Torrefier	To torrefy, scorch with heat
Tournedos	Small, round steak from beef fillet, owing to its thickness not usually cooked in the room
Tranche	Slice, collop, steak or rasher
Tranchelard	Literally larding knife but usually describes long thin carving knife used for hams
Trancheur	Carver, hence chef trancheur
Tranchoir	Trencher, plate.

V

Vésuve	Vesuvius; used (as volcano) in describing flambé form of *omelette* or *soufflé en surprise*
Voiture	Carriage (used to describe restaurant trolley)
Vulcain	Vulcan (god of fire in Roman mythology).

W

Wagon	Waggon (used to describe restaurant trolley)
Whiskey, whisky	Usually Irish whiskey (spelt with "e") and Scotch whisky spelt without
Wisky	French corruption of whisky hence *au wisky*.

X

| *Xérès* | Sherry. |

Z

| *Zeste* | Zest (of lemon, orange, etc). |

INDEX

Abbots Aged Bitters, 24
Abricota, 21
Abricotine, 21
Aquavitae, 23
Advocaat, 21
Akvavit, 23
Alfredo (restaurateur), 47
Almonds, 84, 88; blanched, 30
Amer Picon, 24
Amourette, 21
Anchovies, 41, 45, 130, 135
Angelica, 21
Angostura, 24
Anisette, 21
Appareil à crêpe, 81
Apple jelly, 84; purée, 84; tart, 91
Apples, 63, 73, 88, 90; à pointe, 53
Apricot jam, 88
Apricots, 84, 88
Apry, 21
Aquavit, 19, 21, 23
Armagnac, 19, 23, 61, 65, 74, 75
Arrowroot, 90
Artichokes, 52, 65, 74; à la flamande, 53
Asparagus, 42, 51, 52, 71, 77
Athol Brose, 22
Aubergines, 113; sauté-d, 75
Aurum, 22
Avocada pears, 35

Bacardi, 23, 71, 88
Bacon, 58, 71-3, 114; carving, 106; gammon, 71-3; sauté, 112
Baked Alaska, 116
Bananas, 87-8
Bananes flambé au rhum, 87
Bannerman, Miss Margaret, 85
Barat Palinka, 22
Bar-le-duc jam, 66, 120
Batons de jambon flambés des bons-frères, 73
Bay leaf, 75, 113, 114, 118
Beans, French, 75
Beard, James, 85 n.

Becasse flambée, 64-5
Becassine, 65
Beef, 45-8, 51, 67-70, 77, 100-4, 118; boiled, 29; carving, 92, 94, 105, 106; fillet, 47, 67
Beer, 119
Benedictine, 22, 73, 145
Berti, Mr, 84
Beurre manié, 118
Bicarbonate of soda, 85
Biscuit glacé aux fraises, 89
Bismarck cocktail, 40-1
Bitters, 24
Black cherry jam, 84
Blackcurrant purée, 8
Blackcurrants, 84, 89
Blinis, hot, 107
Blue blazes, 145
Bortsch, 36
Bouchées, 62
Boule de neige, 116
Boulestin, Marcel, 80
Bourbon, 23
Bouquet garni, 59
Brandy, 19, 20, 23, 25, 43, 50, 52, 54, 59, 60, 62, 64, 68, 73, 75, 76, 77, 82, 83, 87, 88, 90, 91, 108, 112, 144, 145; blazer, 145; fine champagne, 23, 62; fine maison, 23; grande champagne, 23; petite champagne, 23; serving, 143-6
Bread, 117, 119, 126-7; black, 46; butter-fried, 51; Danish rye, 46
Brill, 97-8
Brillat-Savarin, 118
Broccoli, 66, 68, 70
Brochettes, 114; de rognons flambées l'armagnac, 114; French type, 113
Brontë, 22
Burgundy, 73, 108
Butter, 37, 41, 42, 43, 44, 46, 47, 48, 49, 50, 51, 59, 60, 61, 62, 63, 64, 65, 66, 68, 70, 72, 73, 74, 75, 76, 77, 82, 83, 85, 87, 88, 89, 103, 110, 114, 117, 119; hot, 110; melted, 52, 81
Buttermilk, 85

Rum, 19, 20, 23, 24, 31, 72, 86, 87, 88, 90, 91; Bacardi, 88; omelettes, 86
Rye, 24

Sabayon, 55
Salade composées, 121; de fruites, 122; de saison, 65; d'orange, 33; simples, 121
Salads, 7, 33, 48, 64, 70, 77, 110, 121–36; Caesar, 130; cheese, 121; compound, 121; décor, 126; dressings, 121–36; equipment for, 18; French, 69; fruit, 53, 55, 121, 122; green, 66, 68, 76, 122–3, 130, 135; plain, 121; potato, 121; shell fish, 121; tossed green, 47; types of dressings, 128–35; wagon for, 123
Salmon, carving, 98
Salt, 29
Satay, 112
Sauces, 52–3, 133; allemande, 50; barbecue, 113, 118; Bourguignonne, 118; Cambridge, 135; chili, 28, 39, 40, 126, 131; crêpe, 82, 83; curry, 132; fish, 60–1; French mustard, 103; Gloucester, 132; Gribiche, 134; homard, 58–9; lobster, 58–9, 61; manufactured, 26–7, 31; Mary Rose cocktail, 38; Melba, 54, 90, 116; oyster, 28; piquante, 49; soy, 27, 28, 51, 103, 126; tobasco, see Tobasco; tomato, 41; wine, 113; Worcestershire, 27, 38, 39, 45, 47, 68, 101, 103, 119, 126, 131
Sauciaux pancakes, 85
Savouries, 26, 56–77, 85, 112, 122
Scaffa, 144
Scallops, 113
Scampi, 44–5, 57, 59, 60; à la crème, 44–5; à la crème Madras, 45; boulevard, 60; flambés à la crème, 60
Schloesser, Frank, 13, 100–1
Schredam, 24
Scotch broth, 27
Seafood cocktails, 28, 33, 38–41, 129; cocktail sauce, 38–9
Seasonings, 126
Sècrestat, 24
Shallots, 43, 44, 47, 50, 51, 60, 61, 68, 75, 77, 118, 129, 130, 131, 134; sauté-d, 51
Shaslik, 114–15; Caucasian, 115; swords, 17–18, 114–15
Shell fish, 43–5, 57, 58–62
Sherbet, 87
Sherry, 25, 38, 43, 44, 50, 52, 58, 66, 71, 76, 101, 110; cooking, 20
Shish kebab flambé, 113. See also Kebabs
Shrimps, 40, 42, 59, 86; cocktail, 40
Side table, 9
Skewered dishes, 112–15
Skewers, 112–14
Slivovitz, 24
Smitane style of cooking, 112
Snails, 107

Snapdragon, 91
Snipe, 65
Sole, carving, 95–7; 95–7; filleting, 7
Sorrel, chiffonade of, 37
Soufflé, 115–16; belle nuit, 116; en surprise milady, 116; en surprise milord, 116; en surprise Norvegiénne, 116; grand succes, 116; jubilee, 116; volcano, 116–17
Soups, 35–8, 58; cold, 35–6; fruit, 35; hot, 37–8; wine, 35
Spaghetti, 41–2; Napoletaine, 41–2
Spanish cream dressing, 132–3
Spices, 61
Spinach, purée of, 73
Spirit stoves, 11
Spirits, 4, 19–21, 23–4, 25, 50, 60, 77, 84; blending, 20–1
Steak, 38, 45, 46–7, 67–9, 77, 103–4; carving, 101–4; Diane, 14, 17, 27, 68–9; minute au poivre, 46–7; monkey-gland, 27, 67–8; tartare, 45–6
Strawberries, 53–5, 83, 84, 89, 90; wild, 54
Sugar, 5, 30–1, 39, 73, 84, 88, 89; Barbados, 31; brown, 31, 89; caster, 30, 33, 35, 48, 53, 54, 81, 82, 86, 87, 88; Demerara, 31, 88; flavoured, 85; icing, 54, 116; lump, 82, 145; sand, 31; spiced, 31
Sultanas, 88, 91
Suprême de volaille, 50; de volaille à la crème, 50; de volaille grand marc, 62; de volaille sous cloche, 107, 110–12
Sweetbreads, 76–7
Sweets, 53–5, 78–91
Syllabubs, 55
Syrup, 30, 73, 88, 90, 145; fruit, 90, 144

Tarragon, 35, 40, 125, 126, 129, 130, 131, 133, 134, 135
Tartelettes flambées, 90–1
Tenderloin of pork Florida, 49–50
Tequila, 24
Terrines, 107
Thompson, Sir Henry, 123–4
Thyme, 113, 114, 118
Thousand Island dressing, 131
Tia Maria, 23, 89, 143
Toast, 117, 119; finger, 119
Tobasco, 35, 38, 39, 40, 45, 72, 126, 131
Tomatoes, 36, 39–40, 41, 42, 47, 50, 58, 59, 60, 61, 69, 72, 74, 75, 77, 113, 121; cocktails, 28; concassé, 36, 39–40, 42, 47, 50, 58, 60, 61, 74, 77; farcies, 69; purée, 59; Scottish, 72
Tourton pancakes, 85
Tranche de gigot flambée, 67
Trout, carving, 98
Truffles, 42, 51, 65, 99, 111, 118; julienne of, 76
Turbot, carving, 97–8
Turkeys, carving, 100